KEEPING CHICKENS

KEEPING CHICKENS

A Kid's Guide to Everything You Need to Know about Breeds, Coops, Behavior, Eggs, and More!

MINDIE DITTEMORE

Sky Pony Press
New York

Sky Pony Press books may be purchased in bulk at special discounts for sales promotion, corporate gifts, fund-raising, or educational purposes. Special editions can also be created to specifications. For details, contact the Special Sales Department, Sky Pony Press, 307 West 36th Street, 11th Floor, New York, NY 10018 or info@skyhorsepublishing.com.

Sky Pony® is a registered trademark of Skyhorse Publishing, Inc.®, a Delaware corporation.

Visit our website at www.skyponypress.com.

10 9 8 7 6 5 4 3

Manufactured in China, 2021
This product conforms to CPSIA 2008

Library of Congress Cataloging-in-Publication Data

Names: Dittemore, Mindie, author.
Title: Keeping chickens: A kid's guide to everything you need to know about
    breeds, coops, behavior, eggs, and more! / Mindie Dittemore.
Description: New York, NY: Sky Pony Press, [2019] | Audience: Age 6-12. |
    Audience: Grade 4 to 6. | Includes bibliographical references and index.
Identifiers: LCCN 2019014677 (print) | LCCN 2019017848 (ebook) | ISBN
    9781510745841 (Ebook) | ISBN 9781510745834 (print: alk. paper)
Subjects: LCSH: Chickens—Juvenile literature. | Pets—Juvenile literature.
Classification: LCC SF487.5 (ebook) | LCC SF487.5 .D58 2019 (print) | DDC
    636.5—dc23
LC record available at https://lccn.loc.gov/2019014677

Cover design by Daniel Brount
Cover photo by Ann Accetta-Scott

Photo courtesies: pages 45, 51, 136, 190: Ann Accetta-Scott; page 78: Cheryl Aker; page 209: Jessica Ashby; page 87: Jennifer Cobb; page 76: Don Converse; page 101 (top): Pamela Estes; page 154: Susan Everett; pages 108, 152: Janet Garman; pages 36 (top), 39, 193: Jessica Gilby; page 46: Melanie Johnson; pages vi, 17 (top): Amber Pardeik; page 210: Veletta Reed

Illustrations and remaining photos by Mindie Dittemore

Print ISBN: 978-1-5107-4583-4
Ebook ISBN: 978-1-5107-4584-1

To my parents, who instilled a love of animals in me, my wonderful family, who puts up with my crazy critter antics, and all my friends and fans who put up with me babbling about chickens, thank you!

CONTENTS

Author Note   ix

1

A PET WITH PERKS   1

2

CHICKEN ANATOMY 101   9

3

BEST BREEDS FOR YOUR BACKYARD   27

4

BRINGING HOME BABY   41

5

FROM FLUFFY BUTTS TO EGG-LAYING MACHINES   65

6

HOME TWEET HOME   77

7

PREDATORS AND PLAYTIME   95

8

WHAT'S FOR DINNER   109

9

ALL ABOUT EGGS   125

10

IS THERE A DOCTOR IN THE COOP?!   145

11

BEHAVIOR AND TRAINING   179

12

MORE FLOCK FUN!   211

INDEX 238

AUTHOR NOTE

Hi! I'm Mindie. I live in Michigan with my husband, two sons, and a backyard full of animals, including chickens. Growing up in a rural area, I had the joy of raising rabbits, chickens, goats, and sheep. I joined 4H and every summer I looked forward to showing my animals at the county fair. For me it wasn't all about winning, it was about seeing old friends and learning new things. Don't get me wrong, the ribbons and trophies were nice, but for me, I just liked spending time with my animals.

Now, many years later, I am so excited that my children get to grow up with amazing animals like chickens too! And while I enjoy teaching my sons about chickens, I love to help other families on their poultry-keeping journey as well. Whether it is giving a poultry talk at a feed store or going shopping for chicks with my youngest son's friend to help him start a flock of his own, I have always enjoyed sharing my knowledge of chickens with others.

I hope you learn and gain your own chicken confidence with the help of this book!

A Pet with Perks

When I was a kid, chickens were something only country folks kept. Now that I have my own children, backyard chicken keeping has become popular and is on the rise, and for good reason! Chickens are fun and friendly, but they give you more than just entertainment and friendship—chickens have become the pet that makes breakfast!

Chickens each have their own personality. They recognize you and will come running to see you, just like other pets. But what sets chickens apart from "normal" pets is not just the eggs they lay. Chickens are hardworking! They spend all day eating bugs, like ticks. They eat weeds and clean up leftovers from your kitchen. And all that eating comes out as great fertilizer for your yard and garden.

Chickens like to cuddle and be petted, if you raise then from chicks. They form families, which you will be part of! They can be trained where to put themselves to bed, along with tricks, just like your dog. Chickens can provide hours of entertainment—watching them interact and communicate is like having a reality show in your own backyard!

But Are Chickens Right for You and Your Family?

Depending on who you talk to, chicken keeping can be easier than owning a dog. But properly caring for any animal requires some work. Chickens don't take up much space, but you will have to tend to their needs every morning and lock them up safe every night. You will need to feed them, give them water, and clean up after them. You will also have to collect eggs.

If your family travels a lot, chickens may not be the right fit for you. Finding someone to chicken-sit can be a challenge. Sharing fresh eggs with your neighbors is a great way to win friends and hopefully a helping hand once in a while when you need it.

But aren't chickens expensive? That depends on you! Chicks themselves are cheap enough. Food for them is not any worse than other pet food. Housing doesn't have to be bought, you can repurpose a shed you already have. Not to mention there are plenty of do-it-yourself projects that can keep cost down versus buying everything new.

Can I Own Chickens?

You will need to check with your city to see if you are allowed to have chickens. A simple phone call to your clerk's office is best done BEFORE you get chickens. The rules about owning chickens depends on zoning and is different in every area. Some towns have guidelines on how many chickens you can have, limits on keeping roosters, and some even spell out exactly where you have to place your coop in relationship to property lines! All of this is important to know before you buy chicks.

But what if you find out you're not allowed to legally have chickens?! You can always try to change the law. Your local government has meetings and you can petition to have the law changed. Make sure to dress nice and prepare to present facts to argue why the law should be changed. Most cities worry about smells, noise, and pest control. Be sure to find out what your town's concerns are and address them with facts. Getting your neighbors to attend meetings as a show of support is a great way to let lawmakers know that it's not just you who wants the law changed.

Have You Ever Held a Chicken?

Most people haven't! While owning chickens is a great idea, you need to do some research first. Local feed stores sometimes have workshops for people interested in getting into backyard chicken keeping. You can also visit poultry shows, like a county fair, to see and experience what it is like to be around chickens.

I recommend finding other backyard chicken keepers. Most backyard chicken keepers love to talk about their flock! They can make recommendations on coop setups, share tips, and help troubleshoot problems. Having a friend who also raises chickens is a great way to learn and you will always have someone who is just as excited as you are to talk chickens with!

Things You Need to Know Before Getting Chickens

When building or buying a coop, the accepted standard is that each chicken needs four square feet of coop space inside and about ten feet of run space outside. Those measurements are for one bird. You will have to figure out how many chickens you want and multiply it by those numbers. Giving them more

space than recommended decreases problems with bullying and boredom.

Our chicken coop is an old shed. While it isn't as fancy or pretty as a store-bought coop, it does give them much more space to live. We free range our flock, so they have about ¼ of an acre to spread out. This gives each bird the chance to do their own thing, get away from each other, and scratch for yummy bugs.

Did you know chickens can live 8–10 years? As hens get older, they lay fewer eggs. If your local laws only allowed a few chickens, think about only getting a couple at a time. That way when your first group of chickens start laying less eggs, you can add a couple newer layers to the flock.

Some breeds of chickens are raised for meat production, while others are better at laying eggs. Some people only keep their laying chickens a couple years and then butcher them to make room for younger, more productive layers. We don't eat our laying hens when they are no longer productive because older hens provide necessary roles in the flock. Because we let them grow old, we have gotten to experience the wonders and dynamics of a multigenerational flock.

Our oldest hen is the boss. Every member of the flock looks to her for leadership. She is the "mom" to everyone. Each chicken plays a role in their family group and older hens can be valuable in keeping the peace in your flock!

CHICKEN MYTHS AND FACTS

MYTH: You need a rooster in order for hens to lay eggs.

FACT: Hens will lay eggs regardless of if a rooster is present. The roosters serve the same purpose as any other mate in the animal kingdom, and that is to fertilize the egg.

MYTH: Chickens are loud.

FACT: Hens are no louder than humans! On average a hen clucks at about 60 decibels. Scientific studies done inside poultry farm buildings during the day range from 50–90 decibels. Those farms have way more chickens than you will have in your backyard. For reference, an average dog barking is around 80–100 decibels.

MYTH: Chickens are dirty and stink.

FACT: Chickens themselves are very clean animals and spend a lot of time preening (taking care of their feathers) and taking dust baths. Chicken poop, on the other hand, can stink and that is why you should keep your coop clean and compost the poop to be used as fertilizer.

MYTH: Chickens attract rodents and predators.

FACT: Chicken feed can be kept in a metal trash can to keep rodents out of your coop. Just because they will eat chicken food too doesn't mean it's the chicken's fault they are there. Let's face it, wild animals are attracted to all sorts of food. They are already in residential neighborhood eating out of trash bins and raiding birdfeeders.

2

Chicken Anatomy 101

Chickens are amazing animals. Sure, they lay eggs, but there is so much more to know about your flock! But where can you learn more? Your local library and the Internet have a lot of information, but you have to be careful to do proper research. Your best bet is to just keep reading this book!

Common chicken keeping terms can be a little confusing at first. Pullet, brooder, lash egg, what? Don't worry, I'll explain them all throughout the book. But for now, we will cover the basics.

Poultry: domestic birds including chickens, turkeys, geese, and ducks, raised for the production of meat or eggs.

Chick: newly hatched chicken.

Pullet: a young female chicken less than a year old who hasn't laid an egg.

Hen: an adult female chicken who lays eggs.

Cockerel: a young male chicken less than a year old.

Rooster: an adult male chicken.

Flock: a group of birds living together.

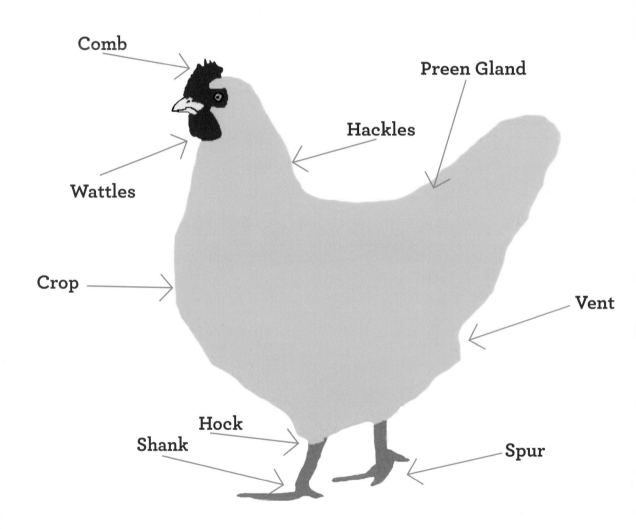

Comb

Preen Gland

Hackles

Wattles

Crop

Vent

Hock

Shank

Spur

Chickens have some of the same body parts we do, though seeing their ears can be a challenge sometimes! And their eyes are way cooler than ours! Not to mention they carry around their own "hair care products." Let's talk about some of the different body parts and what they do.

Comb: the fleshy red growth on the top of a chicken's head which helps regulate body temperature.

Crop: part of the digestive tract that serves as a temporary storage space of food.

Hackles: feathers over the back of a chicken which are pointed in males and rounded in females.

Hock: the "knee" joint of a bird.

Preen gland: an oil sack on the back, near the base of the tail. Chickens use this oil to straighten and clean their feathers.

Shank: the part of a bird's leg between the foot and the hock.

Spur: the sharp protrusion on the back of a bird's leg. Usually found on male chickens, but in some breeds the females grow them, too. Spurs are used for fighting and self-defense.

Vent: the opening in the chicken's bottom where eggs and poop come out. Both the digestive and reproductive systems empty through the vent opening.

Wattle: the flap of skin under the chin of a chicken that helps regulate body temperature.

FASCINATING FACTS
ABOUT CHICKEN EYES

Chickens possess more types of cones than humans do.

They have a cone for ultraviolet light which allows them to "see" shiny bugs and colors like red more easily as they reflect the UV light, versus things that don't reflect the UV light, like dirt.

Chickens also have double cone in their eyes, which enables them to sense slight movements better. This is good for hunting bugs and detecting the fast movements of predators.

A chicken can use each eye independently, on different tasks, at the same time.

Because their eyes are on the sides of their head, chickens have a 300-degree field of vision without turning their head.

In addition to the upper and lower eyelids, chickens have a third eyelid with a nictating membrane. This third eyelid slides horizontally across their eye to protect it from debris. Some reptiles, birds, and sharks also have nictating membranes.

Eyes

Do chickens see better than humans? Yes and no.

Did you know that eyes are made up of these things call rods and cones? Rods are for night vision and cones deal with daytime vision. When it comes to chickens, they have WAY more cones then rods, but what does that mean?

Simply put, did you ever wonder why chickens seem to put themselves to bed at night? Once dusk hits, our flock is always on their roost, and it's because of the low number of rods in their eyes! Because they are diurnal, chickens have evolved with a low number of rods, whereas an owl or say a raccoon has a much higher number, giving it better night vision. So, when it comes to night vision, chickens don't fare any better than we do bumping around in the dark.

But in the daylight, chickens see WAY better than humans. We humans see red, blue, and green wavelengths. Chickens not only have more cones than we do, but those cones are organized within the retina in a mosaic pattern that allows them to see more wavelengths on the spectrum! Chickens even have a cone that can detect violet wavelengths, including some ultraviolet. They also have a specialized receptor called a double cone that scientists believe helps them detect motion. So that's how they get all those bugs!

Comb and Wattles

Both male and female chickens have fleshy growths on the tops of their heads called combs. Wattles are the two oval fleshy growths that hang below their chin. But why do chickens have them?

Have you ever seen a dog panting on a hot summer day? Different animals have different ways of dealing with heat. When your dog's body temperature gets too high, the dog will begin to pant to regulate their temperature. Did you know chickens also pant when they get too hot? They also have a second way to regulate their body temperature—their comb and wattles.

The chicken's blood is circulated through the comb and wattles to help keep the chicken cool in hot weather. The blood is cooled by the air before traveling back through the bird's body. It works just like the radiator in a car! While all combs help with regulating body heat, they don't all look the same. There are several common types of combs.

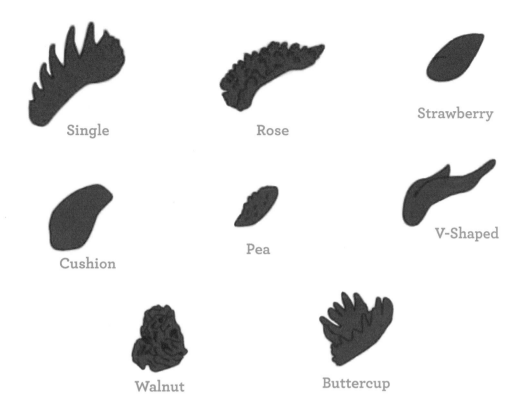

Single

Rose

Strawberry

Cushion

Pea

V-Shaped

Walnut

Buttercup

Single: The single comb is the most common. It is a straight row of spikes starting at the chicken's beak and running back to the back of the head. Breed example: Australorp, Cochin, Rhode Island Red, and Leghorn.

Rose: Rose combs are normally flatter and close to the bird's head. The comb starts at the top of the beak and looks like a cylinder that is covered in wrinkles. Breed example: Wyandottes, Dominiques, and Sebrights.

Strawberry: Strawberry combs are similar to rose combs, except that they form no point and are not as flat. They are bumpy and can resemble strawberries! Breed example: Malays and Yokohamas.

Cushion: The cushion comb is similar to the rose comb, but cushion combs are rounded and smaller. Breed example: Chanteclers.

Pea: The pea comb is one of the smallest types of combs. It has three small ridges of "peas," or bumps. It starts at the top of the head and goes down to the beak. The middle row should be tallest. Breed example: Ameraucanas and Cornish.

V-Shaped: This comb has two distinct sections that resemble the letter "V." They can also look like they have little horns! Breed examples: Houdans, Polish, and Sultans.

Walnut: Walnut combs look like a walnut. They are big, pitted, and round. Breed example: Silkies.

Buttercup: The buttercup comb has a very small single comb in the center, with larger ones on either side. This comb looks like a crown. Breed example: Sicilian Buttercups.

Each comb looks the way it does because of where each breed originated in the world. Chickens with larger combs come from warmer areas of the globe because they need more surface space on the comb to cool their blood quicker. Chickens with smaller combs are from regions where frostbite is an issue.

The comb also helps attract a mate. A large bright comb is a sign of health and strength. The rooster's comb is larger and brighter than that of a hen. It's a way for him to say "look at me, ladies!" But, even among hens, the brightness and size of a comb often plays a part in who is the boss or alpha hen.

Because we now live in a world where things can be shipped globally, you can raise chickens from all over the world! While it is fun to have so many choices, not all breeds of chickens do best in every climate. If you want a healthy flock, you should select breeds that fit well in the climate where you live.

Cold Hardy Breeds

Chickens tend to be generally cold hardy. Most chicken breeds prefer temperatures under 80°F. But certain breeds, such as those with large combs and wattles, or those with smaller body masses, don't do as well in the winter.

Cold hardy breeds for the most part all share some basic characteristics including smaller combs, larger body mass, and the breed having originated in the more northern climates, all of which helps them handle cold temperatures far better than other breeds.

Often the name of the breed is a tip-off. Breeds that have northern states in their names, such as the Rhode Island Red or Delaware, are more cold weather–tolerant.

Ameraucana

Australorp

Brahma

Buckeye

Buff Orpington

Cochin

Delaware

Easter Egger

Jersey Giant

Marans

Plymouth Rock

Rhode Island Red

Sussex

Wyandotte

Heat Tolerant Breeds

Certain breeds, such as those with smaller body masses and larger combs fare better in the heat. Lighter-colored breeds such as Leghorns tend to handle the heat better than darker breeds. Many of the heat-hardy breeds originated in the Mediterranean, go figure!

Appenzeller Spitzhauben	Leghorn
Barred Rock	Polish
Black Sumatra	Rhode Island Red
Brahma	Sicilian Buttercup
Delaware	Silkie
Easter Egger	Sussex
Egyptian Fayoumi	Welsummer

You may have noticed that some breeds made both the cold and heat tolerant lists. Some breeds can handle a wide range of temperatures. Since we live where the temperatures can range from -30°F in the winter to pushing into the 90s in the summer, we pick breeds that span both lists.

Feathers

Think of feathers as your chicken's clothing. Feathers help regulate the chicken's body temperature and protect their skin. Feathers are made of keratin, the same stuff that makes up your fingernails and hair. While a chicken can lose a feather and grown a new one at any time, new feather growth is usually done during molting.

Each feather has a hard, central area called a shaft. Immature feathers have a vein in the shaft and are called pin feathers because they look like pins sticking out of the chicken's skin. These feathers are covered with a thin, white, papery coating that wears off or is groomed off by the chicken. When the cover comes off, the feather expands and the vein in the shaft dries up. A mature feather shaft is hollow and is called a quill.

Feathers grow out of follicles in the chicken's skin. Did you know that around each feather follicle in the skin are groups of tiny muscles? These muscles allow the feather to be raised and lowered, allowing the bird to fluff itself up! To keep feathers in tip-top condition, chickens must be able to take regular dust baths and preen. Good feather growth and maintenance requires proteins, amino acids, minerals, and vitamins.

Types of Feathers

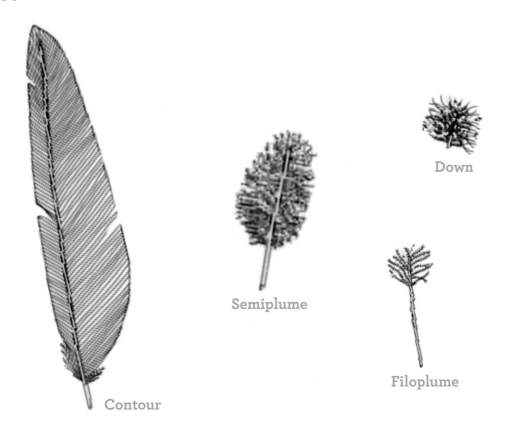

Contour

Semiplume

Down

Filoplume

Down

When a chick hatches, it has a coat of fluffy down. This very fine layer of feathers covers young birds and is found under the contour feathers of older birds. These feathers have a loose structure and trap air, helping to insulate the chicken.

Contour

Contour feathers are the outer feathers that form the chicken's shape and color. These feathers cover the wings, tail, and most of the body. Each contour feather has a shaft with barbs. There are tiny barbules that radiate from the barbs, which lock together to create a strong, smooth feather.

Some breeds have different structured contour feathers that change their appearance. Silkies, for example, have more delicate shafts and long barbs. The barbules are drawn-out and arranged unevenly, giving them their soft feathered and fluffy appearance. Frizzle-feathered chickens have a feather mutation that causes the shaft of the feather to curl or twist. These feathers stick out in a random fashion, like they are having a bad hair day!

Semiplumes

Beneath the contour feathers are semiplume feathers that act as extra insulation. They have a shaft like contour feathers, but not the hooks that hold the barbs together, so they get the soft appearance of down feathers.

Filoplumes

These feather structures are located at the base of each contour feather. Filoplumes are stiff and hair-like in appearance. These feathers don't have muscles around them, but they do have nerve endings that react to help keep the contour feathers in their proper place.

Preen Gland

The preen or urophygial gland is a small bump found at the base of a chicken's tail on their back. The gland produces oil which is rich in waxes and fatty acids. Chickens will collect the oil on their beak and spreads it over their feathers. But why?

Sometimes the barbs on a feather will pull apart, making the feather useless for insulating the chicken's body. A chicken will collect the oil from the preen gland and run the feathers through their beak forcing the barbules to hook back onto the barbs so that the feather can function properly. Not only does the oil help repair the feathers, but it is vital in proper feather cleaning and maintenance. With their own built-in "hair care" products, chickens can keep their feathers in tip-top condition.

Spur

When it comes to the animal kingdom there are predators and prey. Chickens are prey animals—which means other animals eat them. Chickens don't have teeth and can't fight back. Or can they? While chickens aren't equipped with razor sharp teeth, they do have spurs to help them fight.

Spurs are actually part of the leg bone, and they're covered with keratin, the same hard material found in a chicken's beak. They grow, harden, and sometimes curl, developing a sharp tip. Both hens and rooster can have spurs. Rooster spurs are much larger and are an effective weapon for protecting a flock from predators and defending his territory.

When aimed at a human, a rooster's spurs can cause major damage. It's important that if you keep a rooster, you have a plan for how to handle him if he becomes aggressive towards you. Some options for dealing with an overly aggressive rooster is to send him to "freezer camp." That means you butcher him and eat him. You could try to rehome him, but not many people want an aggressive bird. Your best bet is to try showing him who the boss is by carrying him around when you are in the yard.

Usually, spurs require no maintenance. But once in a while, the spurs can grow too long and start to affect the chicken's quality of life. There are different techniques to control spur growth. You can clip, file, and remove the outer growth. Each method has its pros and cons and each chicken keeper has to make their own decision about the best technique to use. But no matter which method you use, the spur will grow back.

3

Best Breeds for Your Backyard

Things to Think about

When it comes to picking out which breeds of chickens might be right for you, keep in mind that the American Poultry Association (APA) recognizes more than 50 breeds of standard size chickens! That's not even counting the bantam size birds! Imagine if you went to a dog show . . . Now replace all those dogs with chickens—bet you didn't know chickens came in so many shapes and colors! So how do you pick the right chickens for you?

First, you have to decide if you want just females or if you don't mind having a rooster. A pullet bin at your local store means that all the chicks are supposed to be female. Hatchery sexing is about 90% accurate. That means you still have a 10% chance of ending up with a male (we have ended up with a rooster out of a pullet bin before). If you want eggs you need hens, which is what a pullet will be when she grows up and starts laying eggs.

A straight run means that there are BOTH sexes in the tub full of fluffy chicks you pick from. Why is this an *oh no* moment? Well, because in our area, by law we are not allowed to keep roosters. The odds of getting a male chicken is way higher in a straight run. And if you aren't allowed to have roosters, you will have to find new homes for the males you get or deal with sending them to "freezer camp."

Another important thing to consider is how many chickens you can realistically home. If you are in an urban setting, this may be governed by an ordinance. Our little town has guidelines as to the number, sex, and housing of chickens within the town limits. Make sure you check your ordinance BEFORE you go buying birds!

Once you know how many you can legally have, keep in mind the general rule is that each chicken needs four square feet of coop floor space and an additional ten square feet of run space per chicken. Of course, if you are bringing home bantam birds, you can squeeze in a few more. You want each bird to have enough room so that they don't start picking on each other out of boredom and confinement. We let our flock free range all day, so we don't have to worry about them not having enough space, but we do have to worry about predators.

Now that you have figured out how many chickens you can handle, you need to think about why you're getting them. Are you looking to collect your own eggs? Are you thinking of raising your own meat? Maybe you want to do both! Different breeds were bred for different reasons.

If you are looking for egg layers, you will want to go with Rhode Island Reds, Leghorns, or Orpingtons (just to name a few). If you are looking to raise your own meat, you will want to pick up Cornish Crosses or Freedom Rangers. Maybe you want eggs and then when production dwindles, you plan to send them to freezer camp. Dual-purpose breeds include Barred Rock, Australorp, and Brahma (among others).

Climate

Does it snow where you live? Is it super-hot year-round? Not all breeds do well in all climates. We live in a colder climate so we keep that in mind when selecting new breeds for our flock. We choose breeds that are cold hardy. We have been known to get down to -30°F and some breeds just can't handle that type of extreme. Since different breeds have adapted to different temperatures, it is important to get breeds that fit where you live.

Keep in mind that if you live in a colder climate, frostbite can be an issue. Chickens with larger combs can develop frostbite on them. Smaller bantam size chickens don't fare as well in colder temperatures either. If you get colder weather, look for breeds that have bigger bodies, smaller combs, and were bred for such climate.

But what about extreme heat? Did you know chickens don't sweat? Chickens regulate their body temperature through their comb and wattles on their head. Most chickens prefer temperatures 80°F or cooler. When a chicken becomes too hot and can't cool off just by circulating blood through its comb, you will see it raise its wings away from its body to help cool off. Chickens can also pant like dogs do to cool down. When chickens start panting, it's not a good sign and it's time to help them with cool treats or even a fan.

See pages 18–21 for more information on what breeds are cold/heat tolerant.

Size

Chickens come in two sizes: standard and bantam. Standard size chickens weigh anywhere from 3–10 pounds depending on the breed. If you want a really big bird, check out Jersey Giants who weigh in at 10–13 pounds. Bantam breeds weigh as little as 1–3 pounds.

Depending on your climate and how much space you have available to house your flock, you might consider choosing bantam breeds. These pint-size balls of fluff are just as cool as their standard counterparts and come in many of the same breeds, just smaller!

Bantams are easier for children to handle because of their size and work well in urban settings with smaller yards. As a rule, you can house ten bantams in the same space that three standard size chickens would occupy. Remember that bantams don't normally come from the hatchery sexed as pullets and cockerels, so it's likely you will end up with some roosters in your flock.

You can keep both standard and bantams in the same flock. There are pros and cons to having bantam birds in your flock. Keep in mind that standard chickens may pick on smaller birds. A standard size rooster may also seriously injure a bantam hen while trying to mate. And while bantam chickens take up less room and eat less, they also produce smaller sized eggs. Just remember that two bantam eggs equal one standard egg.

Egg Color

Chickens come in all shapes and sizes and so do their eggs! Most grocery stores carry white eggs and that's probably what you are used to. And while you may have seen brown eggs too, did you know they come in other colors as well? Marans lay chocolate brown eggs, Ameraucanas lay blueish-green eggs, and Olive Eggers lay darker green eggs. Depending on what breeds you choose, your nest box could look like Easter every day of the year!

Keep in mind the color of the egg shell does not mean one egg is better or healthier for you than another. The pigment put on the eggshell during its production doesn't affect the quality of the egg inside. The myth that brown eggs are "better for you" isn't true.

By now I'm sure your head is spinning with so much to consider when it comes to picking out the best breeds for your backyard. Relax, take a deep breath, and start by looking at a hatchery catalog! While you will likely buy your chicks from a store the first time, many hatcheries have catalogs filled with the breeds they carry. It is fun to look at all the different breeds available. These catalogs list breed characteristics, temperament, and egg production, and are valuable in helping you decide which breeds you like and will work well in your yard.

Keep in mind each chicken is an individual with its own personality. While some breeds are known for being docile and friendly, it is not a guarantee. Buff Orpingtons are widely known for being calm, friendly birds. Not ours! We raised her in our house from a day-old chick and it took forever to get her to calm down. She was flighty and ran from everything, including

Brown eggs

Rhode Island Red
Plymouth Rock
Cochin
Brahma
Jersey Giant
Buff Orpington
Wyandotte
ISA Brown

Very light brown eggs

Silkie

White eggs

Leghorn
Polish

Chocolate Brown eggs

Marans

Green eggs

Olive Eggers

Blue eggs

Ameraucana

us, even though we handled her daily as a chick. Remember to not take it personally and go at the chicken's speed. Our Buff Orpington is now one of the sweetest girls we have, but it took a couple of years of respecting her boundaries and building her trust. She still won't hop up in my lap, but she will let me pick her up without running from me.

Top Breed Picks for Kids

When it comes to chicken breeds, everyone has their favorites, including our family. But when it comes down to chicken breeds that are great for kids, everyone's "Top 10" list is pretty much the same. These are breeds that are calm, friendly, entertaining, and just downright cool to look at!

Australorp

This breed is solid black, although their feathers have a purple and green shine in the sunlight. These chickens are a fast growing, large, heavy bird. They are slightly shy initially, but once they settle in, they are curious, friendly, and outgoing. Australorps lay pale tan eggs and hold the world record for egg laying. When it comes to parenthood, they are good nest sitters and mothers.

Brahma

Brahmas come in both standard and bantam sizes. They are a friendly, calm breed that are used for both meat and egg laying. They do not mind being handled, making them perfect for a 4H project or poultry show. Brahmas come in a variety of colors, have feathers on their feet, and lay brown eggs. Because they are a larger, heavier breed, Brahma hens take a little long to mature before they start laying. They are very suitable for cold climates and make great mothers.

Buff Orpington

Often referred to as the golden retrievers of the chicken world, these buttery yellow birds make a great addition to any flock. Orpingtons are curious, calm, sweet, and friendly chickens. They lay brown eggs and are both cold

hardy and heat tolerant. They love treats and will follow you around the yard.

Cochin

This breed looks like fluffy basketballs. They come in many different colors, and both standard and bantam sizes. Cochins are extremely calm and laid-back. The hens lay large, light brown eggs and tend to go broody (meaning they decide they want to have babies), making excellent mothers. Cochins are easy to handle and quiet. They love to be cuddled and easily become a lap chicken.

Easter Egger

If you want colored eggs, then you'll want an Easter Egger. Though not a recognized breed and often confused with Ameraucanas, these chickens have a genetic trait that causes their eggs to be blue, green, and pink. They come in standard size as well as bantam. They are friendly, curious birds who enjoy

being around their human caregivers. Their appearances can vary, but they typically have very fluffy faces, with puffy cheeks and beards.

ISA Brown

ISA Brown is one of the best breeds for a first-time chicken owner. They are gentle chickens that don't tend to be flighty around children. This great all-around chicken lays LOTS of brown eggs. An ISA hen will lay anywhere from three hundred to three hundred and fifty eggs a year! And they mature earlier than other breeds, so they will begin laying eggs sooner than other breeds in your flock. They are low maintenance and adapt easily to various climates. This breed is extremely sweet and friendly and enjoy interacting with human families.

Polish

Looking like little rock stars, Polish chickens are unmistakable with the pom-pom of feathers on their heads. They are easy for children to catch and pick up because their head feathers can block their vision. If you are worried about their ability to see, the head feathers can be trimmed. While not a great egg layer, this breed makes up for it with their sweet personalities and entertaining antics.

Rhode Island Red

This breed is fun, friendly, and full of personality. They are good layers and thrive in almost any climate. They are usually an extremely healthy breed with long lifespans. While other breeds can survive with minimal upkeep, Rhode Island Reds thrive on little to no upkeep. This makes them ideal for the forgetful child who might not

always perform daily chores to the best of their ability. They are family oriented and do well around children, with the exception of roosters. Rhode Island Red roosters can be fierce when it comes to protecting their flock, and this aggression can turn towards humans.

Silkies

This "ornamental" breed is tiny, lightweight, and easy to handle, making them a great choice for children. Their unusual features include soft, almost fur-like feathers, an extra toe, and black skin. Silkies are not high-volume layers because they tend to go broody. However, their incredible instinct to "mother" makes them perfect for hatching new flock members. Their eggs are about half the size of standard eggs. Silkies are little birds with big personalities.

Wyandottes

This breed is not only beautiful but also incredibly friendly and intelligent as well. They are a dual-purpose breed, kept for their eggs and meat. Their rose-style comb and dense feather covering make them perfect for colder climates. Though they are docile, nonaggressive birds that enjoy being around people on their own terms, they aren't exactly "lap chickens."

4

Bringing Home Baby

Once you have decided how many chickens your backyard can handle and which breeds you would like to raise, you need to figure out where to get your chicks. You can pick them up from a store or breeder, have them mailed to you, or you can hatch them out yourself!

Farm Stores

Most people go to their local farm store during the spring to buy chicks. This is my favorite way to buy chicks since you can see exactly what you are getting. Most stores carry an ever-changing selection of breeds, as they stock what the hatcheries mail them. Most stores have a schedule of what breeds will be in what week, so if you are looking for something specific, don't be afraid to ask.

Since you will be able to choose from the different breeds available, there may be a slight age difference between the chicks, depending on when the store got each breed in. While older birds may pick on younger birds due to their size difference, as long as they are within a couple weeks in age, you should have no problem mixing and matching breeds. One year we got four different chicks of different breeds over a three-week period. While there was a size difference, they all learned to be a family.

When buying your chicks at a store, don't just grab the first few chicks you get your hands on. Take time to watch the chicks, see how they interact with the others in the container. Chickens start establishing a pecking order from the moment they come out of the shell. If everyone is picking on one chick, that chick will always be the "low man." More aggressive chicks will grow up to be alpha hens and run the coop.

You will want to check your chicks over for health. If a chick is just sitting there and you can easily grab it, take heed. Chicks should run from you when you try to pick them up. Make sure their eyes are bright and clear. Make sure their little bottoms are clean too! Chicks can develop pasty butt, which will need to be cleaned, maybe a few times. A clean butt is a good thing! One trick I use for picking chicks is to stick something shiny, like my wedding ring or car keys in the bin of chicks to see how alert they are. You want active and curious chicks!

Mail Order

There are many hatcheries that will sell you chicks online and ship them to your local post office. This is a great way to add specific and rarer breeds to your flock. Many hatcheries begin taking orders in the fall and ordering early has its advantages

when it comes to breed selection. The hatcheries begin hatching ordered chicks in the spring and shipping them out. If you don't order in advance, the breeds available may be smaller as hatcheries only incubate so many extra eggs of each breed.

Depending on the time of year, there may be a minimum number of birds you have to order to ensure they are warm enough while in transit. Be aware that sometimes, depending on the weather at the time the chicks are shipped, the hatchery may include extra chicks for added warmth of the group. These are usually males, but you can try asking that any added chicks be female. Keep in mind the minimum order may be more than you are legally allowed to have in your town.

Mail-order chicks are hatched and put into boxes, then delivered to your post office. It can be a stressful journey and sometimes one or two don't make it. You will also have to be available to pick up your box of birds bright and early. Trust me, while the United States Postal Service has been shipping day-old chicks across the country for over 100 years, your local post office staff doesn't want to have to listen to them cheep all day!

Hatching Your Own

Watching chicks hatch out of eggs is very exciting! With the right tools, hatching your own chicks is a pretty simple process. You will need an incubator and some fertilized eggs. You can buy both online. You can also pick up an incubator at your farm store and eggs from a local breeder.

An incubator is a device that keeps the eggs warm enough for the chicks to grow and hatch. There are different types of incubators, ranging from affordable basic models to more expensive fully automatic ones. Basic still air incubators are affordable, easy to use, and generally work pretty well. You will have to keep an eye on the temperature and humidity and turn the eggs three times a day. Circulated air or forced air incubators cost more, but they also do more. The warmed air is circulated throughout the box by a fan so the heat is more evenly distributed. Many of these come with automatic egg turners so you don't have to remember to turn the eggs.

You will want to get the incubator at least a week before you get the eggs. This will give you time to get it set up properly before you put the eggs in. It is going to be warm and humid inside the incubator, which can breed bacteria. You will want to properly clean the incubator before using it so that your eggs will have a sanitized environment in which to develop. Use a mild dish soap and hot water to make a solution to wipe everything down with.

Once the incubator is clean and dry, place it in an area where temperatures are steady, and where there are no drafts. You will want to turn on the incubator and check to be sure that it has a constant temperature and that the humidity level is correct. The incubator should be set at 99.5°F and 45–50% humidity.

Eggs must be physically turned to keep the developing chick from sticking to the inside of the shell. If your incubator has an egg turner, simply put your eggs in. If you have to hand turn your eggs, I suggest marking them so you know which side should be up. We use a pencil and mark each egg with an X on one side and an O on the other. Start with the X side up—that way when you go to turn them, you can tell which eggs have been turned because the O sides will be up. You don't want to miss turning an egg! Continue rotating between X and O every time you turn. You will need to turn the eggs three times a day until the 18th day. Once the eggs are in the incubator, you should only open the incubator when necessary, like to turn the eggs. Every time you open the incubator you let heat and humidity escape. Opening the incubator too much can affect the eggs.

It takes 21 days for a chicken egg to hatch. You need to understand that not all fertilized eggs will result in a live chick. Three weeks may seem like a long time to wait and wonder if any of your eggs will hatch a chick. Luckily there is a way to check your eggs to see if a chick is developing, and it's super easy to do!

Candling an egg is when you shine a light through the egg's shell to check if an egg is developing or not. You can buy a special candling light at the farm store or make one with a flashlight and toilet paper tube. I sometimes just use the light on my cell phone to do it! At 7–10 days of incubation, you will be able to see if anything is happening in the egg. By this point there should be a reddish sac that holds the embryo and veins around the inside of the egg which nourishe the growing chick. You may also be able to see the developing chick moving! If the egg is clear, it means there is no chick growing inside and it should be removed from the incubator. You should only candle a couple eggs at a time and not keep the eggs out of the incubator for more then 5–10 minutes.

On day 18 of incubation, your eggs will go into "lock down." This means no more turning the eggs and no opening the incubator. At this point your growing chicks are getting ready to hatch and need to be left alone. There is a lot going on inside the egg as they get ready to join the world. The chick will finish absorbing the yolk and begin breaking through the membranes into the air sac in the shell. When it is ready, it will use its egg tooth to break through the shell, called pipping. The egg tooth is a temporary hard, sharp bump on the upper beak of a chick. The egg tooth falls off within days of hatching.

Once you see a pip hole it can take up to 24 hours for the chick to escape the shell. You may begin to hear your chick cheeping once it pips.

Over the next few hours, the chick will begin to zip the egg open by using its egg tooth to make a crack all the way around the shell. This takes a lot of energy and the chick will nap on and off between working. Once the crack is finished, the chick will begin pushing the egg open with its feet. When it comes out of the egg it will be wet and exhausted, but within a few hours it will dry out and begin exploring its world. Once the chicks are dry, they can be moved to a brooder.

Remember, it can take up to 24 hours for a chick to hatch once it pips the egg. It might be tempting to try to help them get out faster, but don't! As they hatch, the blood vessels in the shell need time to dry up. If you try to "help" them hatch you could seriously injure them. Also, not all eggs will hatch exactly at 21 days. It is best to let unhatched eggs have a few extra days. You can try candling them to look for movement before giving up.

Setting Up a Brooder

Before you buy or hatch your baby chicks, you will need to make sure you are ready to take on the role of mother hen. Just like human babies, baby chicks need a nursery. A chicken nursery is called a brooder. It needs to have certain things like food, water, and heat.

You can use a lot of different household items as a brooder. We have used an old guinea pig pen, cardboard boxes, my neighbor once used a children's wading pool, but my favorite is a plastic storage tote. You will want to make sure your brooder box is tall enough to contain your new chicks. They may not be flying now, but give them time and they will be out of your box! Totes are tall enough to keep chicks from getting out and with a little chicken wire for a lid, secure enough that your other pets (cats/dogs) can't get in. Chicks grow fast and keeping them contained is important while they are in your house. While my neighbor's kiddy pool worked at first, her chicks soon grew big enough to hop out of the pool and were running all over her basement!

Make sure your brooder is spacious enough for the number of chicks that will be in it. You don't want the chicks to fight due to lack of space. And remember, the chicks will grow and take up more room over time.

Bedding

You will need to put an absorbent bedding material in the bottom of your brooder. Bedding provides a soft place for chicks to rest, but also helps control droppings. Newspaper is a strict no-no as it doesn't absorb and it becomes slick and could cause injury to your little one's legs. Don't use sand either as it can become too hot, it can be a breeding ground for disease, and little chicks, not knowing any better, can mistake it for food and become sick. Just like human babies, chicks put everything in their mouth as they explore their world.

Until chicks figure out what food is, they can be tempted to try to eat the bedding you use. We usually start off with paper towel till our day-old chicks begin eating well, then switch to a kiln dried pine wood shaving material. Avoid cedar shaving because the fumes from the wood can damage their respiratory systems.

Food and Water

After baby chicks hatch, they absorb their yolk sac, which provides them with all the nourishment they need. This is what makes it possible for hatcheries to mail day-old chicks to stores

or you. After 72 hours, the yolk sacs are gone and they will need food and water.

The first thing your chicks are going to need once they arrive at your home, is water. Chickens require a lot of water. You will need to keep their waterer filled and clean at all times. And let me tell you, chicks can and will kick shavings, food, and poo in their water and gunk it up. They are messy just like any other baby in this world. Chicks can also drown in their water, so make sure you get an appropriate waterer. Waterers come in plastic and metal and are very affordable. Make sure you get the proper chick size and then as they grow you can purchase an adult size waterer. We set our waterer on a board or brick to lift it up off the floor of the brooder, which helps keep the water cleaner and the brooder bedding drier.

For chicks, there are feeds that have been specifically formulated to give growing chicks everything they need. Chick "starter" should have at least 18 percent protein so the chick grows properly. The feed should also include amino acids, prebiotics and probiotics, and vitamins and minerals to support all aspects of your chick's health. If the chicks have been vaccinated for coccidiosis, then the unmedicated feed should be used, while medicated feed is good for chicks that haven't been vaccinated. Ask the store or hatchery if your chicks have been immunized. If you aren't sure if your chicks have been vaccinated, I highly recommend using the medicated feed.

Like any naughty little children, your chicks will pick through and fling their food. Who wants to waste money on food? Placing a piece of cardboard under the feeder will keep bedding out of the feeder as well as catch food they may kick out. If the tiny food falls into the bedding, the chicks usually ignore trying to find it again. But if it is caught on the cardboard, it is still available for them to eat.

Warmth

The brooder needs to be draft-free. Your chicks will need to stay warm, as if their mother were sitting on them, and a draft is counterproductive. Since you are now the chicks' "mom" you must keep your babies warm. We use a simple red bulb heat lamp. The red bulb helps prevent pecking issues and is shown to be less stressful on the birds than a white bulb. I would not recommend using a heat lamp with a cardboard box as it could be a fire hazard. You will also want to make sure the heat lamp is properly secured. They come with a clamp, but that could easily be bumped or knocked down if you only use the clamp. No one wants a fire hazard, so I always recommend a second way to secure your lamp, be it a chain, bungie cord, or whatever else you have on hand.

You will want the temperature under the lamp on the floor of the brooder to be between 90–95°F for the first week. You should decrease the temperature by five degrees each week after that for about 4–6 weeks or till the temperature in the brooder is the same as the temperature outside. You can do this by raising the heat lamp up. We place the lamp at one end and the food and water at the other end of our brooder. This gives the chicks the option of getting away from the heat if they are too warm. You will see them panting if they are too warm and have no way to get away from the heat. When the chicks are cold, they will huddle together in a pile under the lamp. Pay attention to your chicks' behavior and adjust the heat as needed.

Safety

Make sure your brooder is set up for safety, not just from the inside, but from the outside too. If you have other pets, make sure the brooder is set up somewhere they cannot get access to it. Trust me, even if you think your cat or dog would never hurt the chicks, think again. While I love our dog, I have no doubt in my mind, given unsupervised time, she would snarf a chick in a heartbeat. Our cats, while calmer around the chicks, have been known to try to bop them on the head.

And don't forget about very young children. Baby chicks are SO cute, but they are very delicate too. Make sure young children can't get into the brooder and are supervised till they know how to properly and gently handle chicks.

Enrichment

Just like all babies, chicks need to be stimulated. Who wants to just sit in a box all day? You can include a small roost in your brooder box, along with a small dust bath area, and even a mirror. We even give our chicks some

of the children's toys to spice things up, like Mega Bloks and matchbox cars! Be creative and keep food treats to a minimum.

If you do provide your chicks with a few snacks, make sure you hand-feed them. This will help assure your chicks grow up to be friendlier, running toward you instead of away from you! Make sure snacks, like grapes, are cut up into small pieces to avoid choking. Remember, you want your chicks to fill up on feed that is packed with nutrition, not snacks.

Cleaning

You need to be prepared to clean as well. For what goes in those adorable little beaks will come out those cute fluffy butts. You should tidy the brooder daily by scooping out the poo and any wet shavings. As the chicks get older, they will start to smell more and more. Instead of spot cleaning the messes, you may have to totally clean out your brooder every day. Using a plastic tote makes for easy cleanup with a simple dumping of the contents and a quick scrubbing in the bathtub. Keeping the brooder clean and dry is important for healthy chicks.

If you keep these basics in mind when setting up your brooder, you will provide your chicks with the best start possible in life. Remember that chicks are babies. They are fragile and sleep a lot. Try not to disturb and handle them when they are sleeping. They need their rest to grow into strong, healthy, egg-laying machines. If you are handling a chick and it falls asleep in your hand or on your chest, enjoy the moment—they trust you enough to nod off! Chicks grow fast, and before long, you will be making little trips outside with them, getting them ready for the big world beyond the brooder!

How to Handle Chicks

Chicks are babies, which means they are fragile and can get hurt if not handled properly. You should play with them to help make them friendly, but just be careful with those little balls of fluff. When picking up a chick, always scoop it up from underneath. Place your other hand over the chick's back to keep it from

jumping or falling out of your hands as you walk to where you plan to spend time with your chick.

It is best to place a towel on your lap or have paper towels nearby when handling chicks. Just like human babies, baby chicks don't use a toilet. Chicks don't really care where they do their business and will give you little "gifts."

You should keep your playtime short as your babies will get tired fast. Chicks also get cold quick, so either return them to the heat of your brooder, or let them snuggle up to you for warmth. Chicks can move fast, so handle them one at a time so you don't have one disappear on you.

When handling your chicks, it is good to talk to them. They will learn the sound of your voice and it is a good time to start teaching them their names. Yes, chickens can learn their names! Remember to talk soft, move slow, and be gentle when spending time with your new babies. And remember to wash your hands when you are done handling them.

Sexing Chicks

When purchasing chickens from a hatchery or feed store, remember that even the most reliable sexing methods they use have a margin of error. Maybe you hatched your own chicks and are wondering when you will know if you have boys or girls. While there are many old wives' tales that claim you can predict or test for gender, they just aren't dependable.

The easiest way to tell a chick's gender is to wait and see. By three weeks of age, chicks start to physically change. If you have all of the same breed, if you have any roosters, you will notice their features are larger than that of the females.

Some of the physical features you can use to determine sex include:

Comb and Wattles: In general, males have larger, darker combs and wattles then female chickens. If you notice one chick's comb and wattles appear to be developing at a faster rate than the other chicks, it is a good indicator that it is probably a male.

Hackle Feathers: These feathers grow around a chicken's neck area. A female has shorter, rounded feathers. Males have longer and more pointed feathers.

Tail Feathers: Males of most breeds have larger, longer tail feathers than their female counterparts.

Feet and Legs: Males tend to have bigger feet and longer, thicker legs.

Some breeds can be sexed by the color of their down at hatching. These breeds are called sex-linked. It means you can tell males and females apart by how they look at birth. These are hybrid chicken breeds and are not recognized by the American Poultry Association, so would not be a good breed to get if you're interested in showing your chickens in poultry exhibitions.

Of course, if your chicken crows, you can be pretty sure it is going to be a rooster. I say "pretty sure," because we have a hen that crows! She is an Easter Egger and lays some of the most beautiful blueish green eggs you have ever seen, but every morning she gets up and crows when she leaves the coop.

My Chick Is Sick!

You are likely to never encounter health problems with your new baby chicks beyond the occasional pasty butt. But there are things that can go wrong and knowing what to look for and how to handle them if they do ever happen is important.

Pasty Butt is when a chick has poop stuck to its butt. The poop hardens and plugs the chick's vent, making it impossible for them to go potty. This can be a fatal condition if the vent is not cleaned. Treating Pasty Butt

is very easy, so don't worry. First and foremost, *do not* pull the poop off, as it will rip off feathers and skin, causing major injury. Fill a sink or bowl with warm (not hot) water, and wet a paper towel so you can drip the water on to the rock-hard poop. You should notice the blockage start to soften so it can be gently removed. Continue wetting the area and removing the dried poop till the vent area is clean. When you have gotten the area clean, dry off the chick and place it back in the brooder. Keep an eye on the chick, as it can develop pasty butt again.

Coccidiosis is the number one cause of death in baby chicks because it is highly contagious. This is a parasitic disease of the intestinal track caused by coccidia, which thrives in moist, warm conditions, like a dirty brooder. That is why it is so important to keep your brooder clean. Some symptoms you may notice is that your chick is sluggish and they have bloody stool.

If any of your chicks have bloody diarrhea, they need to be separated immediately. Remember, this is a highly contagious disease. However, there are medications that can successfully treat this condition. The most common drug in treating coccidiosis in backyard settings is Amprolium. It can be mixed in the water and is used for 3–5 days for successful treatment. It is sold at most farm stores but under brand names. Ask your store staff for help locating it. If you can't find it in a store, you may have to call a vet.

Coccidiosis wreaks havoc on the digestive tract, killing the good bacteria that lives there too. Once you have successfully treated your sick chicks, you can give them a little plain yogurt to help rebuild their gut health. While chickens don't process dairy products very well, the live cultures in the yogurt are valuable to intestinal health, so a little won't hurt them. You can also sprinkle a little probiotic powder in their feed to help rebuild the good bacteria.

Stargazing, also called wry neck, is a condition where a chick is unable to hold up its head properly. Chicks grow fast and a lack of the right vitamins and electrolytes can cause them to develop this problem. The symptoms of this condition include lack of energy, not wanting to eat or drink, loss of balance, and falling down.

Poultry vitamins and electrolytes are easily found at most feed stores and can be added to the chick's drinking water. These supplements can be used as a preventative for this condition, and they can also be used to treat it. Many poultry keepers use Brewer's yeast too, which can be sprinkled on the chick's food. Make sure to keep an eye on an affected chick to make sure they are eating and drinking and not being trampled by the other chicks in the brooder.

Respiratory or breathing issues can be a problem in chicks. Chickens have complex respiratory systems and are vulnerable to breathing problems. While there are serious breathing illness, more likely than not at this age your chicks are simply being bothered by something in the brooder.

Never use cedar shavings in a brooder as the oils and scent can irritate your chicks' lungs and sinuses. Make sure if you use pine wood shavings as bedding, that it is made up of larger sized pieces as to cut down on the dust level. Also, when cleaning your brooder use white vinegar instead of bleach, because bleach mixed with the ammonia in chick poop can create a toxic fume.

Separate the sick chick into an area that is low in dust and other possible irritants. You can try to clean the eyes and nostril areas with saline solution, but be careful not to use too much as you don't want them getting it in the lungs. You can find saline in the eye care section of most pharmacies. A little dribble should do. If symptoms don't clear up in a few days or continue to worsen, then your chick could be suffering from a more serious illness and you should contact a vet.

Spraddle Leg is a condition where one or both legs slip out to the side, making the chick unable to stand or walk properly. This condition can be caused due to incubator temperatures fluctuating or being too high. It can also happen to young chicks if the brooder floor is too slippery. This is why you should not use newspaper in your brooder. Spraddle leg can also be the result of a vitamin deficiency.

To treat spraddle leg, you can start by adding vitamin supplements to your chicks' water. Next you will need to stabilize the chick's leg by using some vet or sports wrap around the legs (above the knees) to help keep the legs in place for a few days. This is called a hobble splint and will allow the legs time to build up muscle tone and strength.

Curled Toes can be cause by an injury or a vitamin deficiency. Remember, chicks grow fast and their bodies need a lot of vitamins to grow properly. You will notice that the chick's toes are curled under and it is walking on its foot like a fist. Don't worry, it looks worse than it is.

You can correct curled toes by adding vitamins to the water and by creating a corrective "shoe" for them to wear. Simply cut a thin piece of poster board or similar material in the shape and size of the foot when the toes are uncurled. This will give the toes some resistance, keeping them stretched out, but not so much as to be painful. Cut a piece of gauze the same size to create padding for the "shoe." Place a strip of vet or sports wrap on the table with the poster board and gauze on top. Uncurl the toes and place the chick's foot on top, securing the "shoe" around the foot with the wrap.

Scissor Beak or Crossed Beak is a birth defect where the top and bottom of a chick's beak don't line up properly. It is most likely genetic and will get worse as the chick grows. This condition will affect the chicken's ability to eat and drink, but there are things you can do to help it lead the best life possible. You can gently use an emery board to file down the beak to help it close better. You can also move the water and feed dishes to shoulder lever making it easier for the chick to drink and scoop food instead of pecking at it.

Marek's Disease is a highly contagious disease. This disease causes tumors to grow inside and/or outside of the chick. The iris of their eye will turn gray and will no longer respond to light. Chicks will also become paralyzed. Sadly, there is no treatment for this disease and it has a high death rate. If a chick does survive, it will be carrier of the disease, meaning it can infect other birds. While there is a Marek's vaccination offered by many hatcheries, it is not 100% effective.

5

From Fluffy Butts to Egg-Laying Machines

Ages and Stages

Over the first six weeks of your chicks' lives they will grow from fluffy little balls to awkward teens. Within six months they will be full grown adults. Time moves fast for your flock the first year and it's good to know what's going on.

In the Brooder

When you first bring home your new chicks, they will be covered in fluff. They may even still have their egg tooth on their beak that they used to hatch out of the egg. Newly hatched chicks sleep A LOT. Just like human babies, "infant" chicks will eat and sleep most of their first week. While brand new chicks are extremely adorable and you will want to cuddle them often, they need their rest to grow big and strong. Trust me, watching sleeping chicks can become addictive. There is nothing so sweet as a little ball of fluff snoozing away.

During their first and second week of life, the chicks will start developing wing feathers. They will also become much more active. Expect them to be a little scared of the big world beyond their brooder box, but enjoy spending more time with them as they become curious and begin exploring the world. Even this young, chicks start to display instinctual behaviors like scratching the ground while eating and trying to dust bathe. Of course, just like human toddlers, your chicks will be awkward in these behaviors.

By week three your chick's tail feather will begin to sprout. They will start perching. They may even begin to fly out of the brooder! Just like young children, they are full of energy and curiosity. They love to explore and are quickly moving towards adulthood.

At just a month old, your chicks will begin to go through the "teenage" phase. Just like human teens, your chicks will look awkward and scruffy as their growth explodes! They will have lots of feathers coming in and their comb and wattles will become larger. You'll be able to tell if you have any roosters in your brooder because their combs and wattles will be larger then everyone else's.

At six weeks old, your cute, fluffy chicks have turned into fully feathered young adults. They will continue to grow and fill out, looking less awkward. Imagine they are the human equivalent of a high school senior. They are on the verge of heading off to college or, in the chicken's case, outside. They think they are grown and ready to face the world but deep down they are still finding themselves and their place in the world.

Moving Outside

At some point all parents have to let their children head out into the world. At six weeks old, your chicks are now chickens and ready to head out to the coop. As long as your temperatures are warmer (60°F) and consistent, your flock will do just fine.

Make sure you show them around their new home, pointing out where to get water and food. Place them on the roost so they know where to go at night. Trust me, you will probably have to place them on the roost at night for a while until they learn the routine, but they can and will learn. Our flock puts themselves to bed every night because they learned that's where they need to be when dark falls.

When you first take your flock to the coop, make sure you spend time with them. You want to be sure that none of them get into any kind of trouble that you didn't think about. Give them a day or two to explore their new coop before letting them head out into their run or before letting them free range. If you do plan to free range your flock, you might want to trim their wing feathers on one side so that they can't hop over fences as well. Young chickens can be skittish or too brave for their own good and end up places they shouldn't be!

How to Trim Wing Feathers

Chickens can't fly as well as other birds, but they can flap their wings to get enough lift to get over fences, out of the coop, or out of your yard. If you've got backyard free range chickens, clipping their wings is a must so that your chickens don't escape and get lost, or worse, into danger. You usually only have to trim the wing feathers once or twice before the chicken learns where it should stay. Clipping a chicken's wing might seem a bit scary if you've never done it before, but it really isn't as difficult or dangerous as you may think.

The first step in trimming a chicken's flight feathers is actually catching the chicken. This is the hardest and most time-consuming part. Some chickens are docile and like being touched, others fear humans and run away. A few things that seem to help is to corner them in a small space so they have less of an area to get away from you. You can also use a towel and throw it over the chicken. That should slow them down enough for you to grab them. I've found the easiest way to catch a chicken is to use treats to get them to come to you.

Once you have the chicken in hand, turn it over on its back. When a chicken is on its back it goes into a trance of sorts, and will be much easier to handle. If you have someone who can hold the chicken while you trim the feathers, it doesn't matter if the chicken is on its back or not. Once the chicken is secured, gently pull the wing out to expose the primary flight feathers. You can tell the primary flight feathers because they are generally longer and are the first ten or so feathers closest to the tip of the chicken's wing.

Use a pair of scissors to cut the primary flight feather about halfway to two-thirds of the way down. The idea is to cut off a significant amount of the feathers, without causing the chicken to bleed. Think about when you trim a dog's toenail, you want it  short, but not so short it bleeds. If you do happen to make your chicken bleed, don't get upset. Apply pressure to the area with a towel and then put corn starch on the cut feather to help slow the bleeding and help it clot. When done right, your chicken feels nothing. Just go slow, taking off a little at a time if you're nervous.

We only clip one wing on each of our new chickens. The idea behind clipping just one wing is that the chicken will be thrown off balance. Some chicken keepers clip both wings. I think it depends on the chicken! If you clip one wing and the chicken still figures out how to get enough lift to get out, you will have to clip the other side as well.

When your chickens molt and grow new feather, you will have to repeat the process if you notice any naughty behavior from your flock.

Laying and Eggs

Your fluffy little chicks have grown up and moved out, so now what? Depending on which breeds you have will determine how soon they lay. Some breeds, such as the Golden Comets, have been bred specifically to lay lots of eggs. They may begin laying as early as 16 weeks. The downside of these egg intense breeds is they have a much shorter life span. Laying eggs takes a lot out of a hen!

Breeds like the Rhode Island Reds and Barred Rocks usually begin laying around 18–20 weeks. On average, a female chicken starts laying eggs at about 24 weeks, or 6 months, of age. However, there are some heavier breeds that can take up to 28 weeks before they produce an egg. Each chicken is an individual and like

people, we all get where we are going in our own time. It may seem like it takes forever to get your first egg, but it will come.

You can tell when your pullet is about to start laying because her small pink comb will get larger and redder. She will become more vocal in preparation for singing her first "egg song." She will start checking out possible nesting areas and even try sitting in the nest boxes for short periods of time. Her pubic bones will become more flexible and begin to spread apart to make room for the eggs to pass.

From a hen's point of view, laying an egg is all about producing chicks. A hen will begin to squat if a rooster approaches so they can mate. If your flock has no rooster, she may squat if you attempt to pet or touch her. Catching a chicken becomes a lot easier when she begins to lay because they will usually squat when approached.

Most chickens live an average of 7–8 years with peak egg production around 18–24 months. After 24 months, egg production tends to drop. Hens will continue to lay as they age, but may not lay quite as many eggs.

Old Age

When you first get chickens, few people think about what will happen when their hens become older and no longer lay, but you should. Although a hen will stop laying eggs as she ages, she still has an important place in the flock. Many older hens fill the role as the leader of the flock. They teach younger hens all about flock life and help keep the peace of the pecking order.

Our older hens are important in teaching the new girls how to build a proper nest, where to roost, where the best bugs are, and how to hide from predators. They teach the younger ones what treat time is and show them that human interaction leads to good things. They can also still provide poop, which makes amazing fertilizer for a garden.

Challenges of Keeping Older Hens

One of the biggest issues for older birds is mobility and agility. Many older birds suffer from arthritis as they age, but there are simple things you can do to make life easier. The first is to make sure that food and water containers are easy to get to. This might also mean providing food and water inside and outside the coop so they don't have to walk as far to get what they need.

You can lower roosts or add ramps and ladders to them and to nesting areas, making it easier for older chickens to get where they need to go. Our coop has really high perches but we have different level areas for them to hop up on and easily get where they want to go. As long as your hen can get around, eat/drink, and appears otherwise content, enjoy the time you have with them.

Saying Goodbye

Sadly, part of owning any animal is saying goodbye. Sometimes a chicken gets ill or is taken by a predator, but the lucky ones simply grow too old. As your chickens near the end of their lives you will notice their combs and wattles begin to shrink while their legs and feet become thicker. They are less active and stop laying eggs. A long life for a chicken may not seem that long to us, and while it may not feel very fair, know that you gave them the best life you could.

You have raised this chicken, you named it, posted photos of it on social media . . . it is okay to be sad. Your flock will be sad too. When a chicken nears the end of their life, they just seem to know, as do the other members of the flock. When our hen Goldie was near the end of her life, she found a nice quiet place by herself. The other members of the flock took turns visiting

her and sitting with her as if saying their goodbyes. After I brought her in the house for her final hours, the flock walked around looking for her. It was sad, but it was nice to know they cared as much about her as I did.

Your flock will recover and rebuild the pecking order because life goes on. It's a sad fact of life. And while your heart might be breaking too, just remember the good times you had with your amazing feathered friend.

6

Home Tweet Home

Chickens need a clean, safe coop with enough room for everyone to fit comfortably. Each chicken needs four square feet of coop floor space. Remember this is their house where they will eat, sleep, lay eggs, and hang out during bad weather. They each need to have enough room so that they don't start picking on each other out of boredom and confinement.

You will also need an additional ten square feet of run space per chicken. The run is their yard where they can go out and look for bugs, exercise, and just enjoy being a chicken. A run is an enclosed, fenced-off area that the chickens use during the day. Some people let their chickens free range instead of building a run. There are pros and cons to both runs and free ranging, which we will look at in the next chapter.

It's All about Location

If you ask anyone buying a house, they will tell you it's all about location. Chickens are no different! Of course, you have to keep in mind any local laws or rules about coop placement. Some towns have rules about how far from the property line or other buildings the coop must be. Once you figure out where you can't put it, you need to look at the areas left.

Your coop should be on a flat area with good drainage. No one want to live in a muddy puddle! The coop should get some sunlight through the day but also have some shade to keep your chickens cool in the summer. If your yard doesn't have trees, you can plant bushes in the chickens' run area for them to hide under to cool off. If it snows where you live, you will also want to take into consideration how far from your house you are willing to walk while carrying water on nasty days. You should also place your coop where you can easily see it from a window of your house to make checking on them quick and easy. I know I enjoy looking out and watching them go on about their lives.

Styles of Chicken Coops

Just like there are many different styles of homes we can live in, there are different types of coops you can buy, build, or convert for your chickens. Some coops are permanent structures, while others can be moved. No matter which type of coop you end up picking, it needs to be built sturdy enough to handle whatever weather your area gets and defend against predators. It should have good ventilation, and secure doors and windows.

Our coop is an old gardening shed that is attached to the back of our garage. It was never meant to hold anything more than a few gardening tools and a lawn mower. But with a few simple additions to this bare space, it became a perfect spot for our chickens, ducks, and rabbits to live! You really don't have to spend a lot of money to make a comfortable home for your feathered friends. Many coop designs can be built from scratch, but if you're not handy, you can always buy a premade coop—just make sure the coop has the proper space needed for the number of chickens you plan on having. It is always a good idea to have more space because raising chickens can be addictive and your flock may grow over time.

Small coops are great to start with if you only have a few chickens. Many are available pre-built or as ready-to-assemble kits either online or at local feed stores. You can also find a lot of free coop designs online if you plan to build your own. Many smaller coops are mobile, meaning they are lightweight enough to move or have wheels on them to make moving them easier. The advantage to having a smaller coop is that you can occasionally relocate the coop so that your chickens don't destroy your yard in one area if you are using a run. Moving your coop can also cut down on health issues. Unfortunately, many smaller mobile coops aren't as predator-proof or weatherproof as they should be.

If you end up outgrowing a smaller coop by adding to your flock later, you can still use the smaller coop for isolating sick chickens, as a nursery for a broody hen, or as a grow-out pen for new chickens to help them integrate into the flock safely. Don't feel like you have wasted money by starting with a small coop.

Larger coops are also available pre-built, or you can build yourself. Some of these are even semimobile, meaning the coop is on skies or wheels and can be moved using a truck or tractor. A larger, permanent coop has its advantages in that they are usually built sturdier and are better at protecting your flock from predators. With a permanent coop and run set up, be aware that over time the grass in your run will slowly disappear without proper maintenance, due to normal chicken behavior such as scratching and pooping. Cleaning and reseeding regularly can help keep the run lush and enjoyable for your flock.

Not all coops require building or buying! Other options include converting a shed like we did, converting a portion of your garage, or by enclosing an area in your barn, such as a stall. While you want your coop to fit into your yard and look nice, your chickens really could care less if the color matches the house or if it has ornate peaks or cute shutters on the windows. What matters to your chickens is location, space, and the "furniture" inside.

Every Coop Needs . . .

Beyond the four walls and roof, your coop needs a few basic things to keep your chickens happy and healthy. One of the most important is to make sure the coop is free of drafts. Just like wild birds, chickens have adapted over time to deal with things like cold weather. Here in Michigan we get below zero-degree weather often in the winter. While our chickens do well with the temperature, it is the drafts or blowing winds that cause issues. No one enjoys a cold wind on an already cold day.

What your chickens do need is ventilation. Ventilation is fresh air that can be brought into the coop by opening doors and windows when it is nice out. You can also add ventilation vents near the top of your coop that will allow for air to move out, taking the ammonia from the chickens' poop out too.

While having a window in a smaller coop might seem silly or extravagant, a window provides not only ventilation into the coop, but light as well. Light is very important in stimulating chickens to lay eggs. I have often found the window in our coop is a boredom-buster on rainy days and in the winter. We have a workbench in front of the window and our flock will sit and look out the window on days when going outside is not ideal.

Of course, your coop will have a door for the chickens to use, but there should also be suitable access for humans too. Every inch of your coop will need to cleaned from time to time. By planning ahead and having good access, cleaning will be much easier when you don't have to bend down, crawl around, or turn in funny positions to reach things. Keep this in mind as you plan your coop and begin putting in the items your flock will need.

Food and Water

Your flock will need to have access to food and water. Just like in a brooder, having both slightly raised up from the floor will ensure your flock doesn't waste, spill, or muck up their meals. Both feeders and waterers can be hung or placed on elevated platforms. We prefer to elevate versus hang because our coop is

large and our flock is very active inside during the winter and we would hate for any of them to injure themselves on a chain or rope as they jump and fly to different areas.

We also keep a metal trash can in our coop for storing the chicken food in. We place the bag in the can before we open it so that the food stays dry and secure. No one wants to attract unwanted dinner guests! By keeping your chicken food secure, you are less likely to have unwanted visitors and you will save money by not feeding all the wild creatures in your neighborhood.

Roost Area

Like their wild bird cousins, chickens roost at night—it is an instinctual behavior meant to keep them safe. That is why it is important that your coop has a place for them to roost. Unlike their wild counterparts, chickens do not grip the roost but prefer to sleep flat footed. Your chickens will seek out the highest spot they can find in the coop to sleep, so make sure that the roosting area is higher than the nest boxes so they don't sleep and poop in the nest boxes.

A roost area should have flat "bars" that are 2–4 inches wide. You can easily make your roost bars from a nice piece of 2x4 lumber. Roost bars should be placed at least a foot from the wall and be spaced about 2 feet from the next bar, if you have multiple bars, so that each bird has enough space. Each chicken should be allowed 2 feet of space on the roost in order for them to sit comfortably next to each other. This is helpful in the winter so that the chickens can cover their feet with their fluffy bodies and keep their toes nice and warm, thus avoiding frostbite.

Avoid using round, narrow, or slippery materials such as PVC or dowels for roosting bars. These surfaces and shape require more balance on your chickens' part and put pressure on their feet which can cause foot injuries. Who wants to try to sleep like that?

Chickens poop a LOT when roosting and sleeping. The area under your roosts will accumulate poop. Some chicken keepers use a dropping board. A dropping board under the roosting bars does exactly what you think it does, it catches chicken poop. There are different ways to set them up but the idea is that is makes weekly cleanup easier.

We let our chickens poop directly onto the coop floor in the litter and then shovel it out as needed. During the winter months we use the deep litter method. This is where instead of cleaning out the litter on a weekly basis, you simply put down clean straw or shavings on top of the mess. Why would you do that? Because as the poop and litter break down and begin to decompose, it produces heat, which can help keep the coop floor warmer.

Nest Box

For many chicken keepers, the long wait for the first egg is nerve-wracking. Day after day, you peek in the nest box, waiting with anticipation. When it comes to collecting eggs, you don't want to get an egg with dirt, or worse, poo, on it. But how do you keep your eggs from getting soiled? It's really simple and easier than you might think! It is all about keeping your nest box in tip-top, laying condition.

When it comes to placing your nest boxes, you need to think like a chicken, then you need to act like a keeper. What I mean is, look at laying time through your hen's eyes. If you can't imagine, let me paint you a picture . . .

You're standing in the yard and are gripped by the sudden urge to push. You know it's going to take a little work to get that egg out, so you start looking for a nice, quiet, comfy spot to relax and get to work. I mean, who wants to lay their egg in a nasty, hard, dirty spot in front of everyone? You run in the coop, looking for the perfect spot to lay your beautiful egg, only to find a line for the nest box!

It's kind of like having to use the restroom at a football game. Nobody wants to do private business in a dirty place with a bunch of other people! So how do you keep your hens happy? Read all about it on the next page!

BOXES PER BIRDS: The rule of thumb is one box for every five birds. If you have more chickens than that and only one box, you run the risk of someone needing to lay with nowhere to go, which can lead to pushing and fighting in the box (aka, broken eggs), or your hen will lay somewhere less than ideal. We like to have lots of options for our girls. You will notice though, that there is a favorite spot that all the girls will want to use and most of the eggs will end up all in the same spot.

LOCATION, LOCATION, LOCATION: Position your nest box between the floor and the ceiling but BELOW your roosting area. Keeping the box off the ground assures you have less scratching activity going on in the box. Keeping it below the roost level will keep your birds from sleeping and pooping in the box as chickens will want to roost at the highest point possible.

PROVIDE AMBIANCE: Now if you were a chicken, would you really want to have to lay your egg in a bright, high-traffic area with everyone looking on? No! Well, your chickens don't want to either. Locate your nest box in a quiet area away from the hustle and bustle of the food and water. Chickens like to "hide" their eggs, so make sure the box is in a dimly lit area. If you ever wondered about those crazy chicken keepers who put curtains on their nest boxes and wondered if the hens really like them . . . yes, they do, and this is why!

CONTENT COUNTS: No chicken wants to park their fluffy butt on a hard surface when they lay an egg. Hens will seek out the softest place they can find in order to relax and do their business, so make sure your nest box is that spot. You can use straw, but wood shavings work too. The box just needs to have something soft that will help relax the hen and protect the egg from breaking when it comes out.

SIZE MATTERS!: Bigger isn't always better when it comes to nest boxes. A nest box should accommodate only one chicken at a time. Less activity and jostling in the box means there is less likelihood an egg will break. A good size nest box is a foot by a foot or slightly bigger for larger breeds. Chickens like to feel hidden when they lay and a smaller box is snug and reassuring.

CAN YOU WASH IT?: You nest box should be made out of a material that is easily washed and disinfected. Wood boxes are fine, but can harbor parasites and bacteria even after a good cleaning. By using a metal or plastic nest box, you can give it a more proper cleaning.

CLEAN IT: It is a good idea to clean the bedding in your nest box about once a week. Not only will it be more inviting to your girls, but it will decrease the likelihood of mites. Cleaning it weekly will provide your girls with a clean and dry place to relax while popping out those eggs.

Coop Cleaning

Just like you have to clean your house on a regular basis, your chicken coop will need tidying up from time to time. The roost bars will need to be scrapped. The area under the roost will need to be tidied. Nest boxes will need to be refreshed weekly. Feed and water dishes should be cleaned regularly. Remember, it is up to you to keep your flock healthy.

When cleaning your coop, it is best to use more natural cleaners. Chickens can be sensitive to harsh chemicals in cleaning products. Instead of bleach, use a vinegar solution for scrubbing things down. Once your coop is cleaned and scrubbed down, make sure to let it air dry completely before adding new floor litter and nest box material.

Many chicken keepers sprinkle diatomaceous earth, also referred to as DE, on their coop floor and in nest boxes before adding in new straw and wood shavings. DE is a nonchemical approach to pest control. The fine powder absorbs the oils and fats from the insects, causing the insects to dry out and die. DE is widely used in gardening as well for this reason.

As you clean your coop, it is important to keep your eyes open. Cleaning time is the perfect time to take note of things that need repairs and items that should be replaced.

To Heat or Not to Heat?

We all want the animals we care for to be happy and healthy. Many chicken keepers worry about the comfort of their flocks in the dead of winter. Remember that chickens are birds and just like their wild cousins, they have evolved and are capable of handling cold temperatures. Chickens fluff up their feathers in order to trap warm air close to their body. The flock will also huddle together for warmth.

So, the question remains, to heat or not to heat your chicken coop? Each chicken keeper must make their own choice. For us, we have to weigh the pros and cons of doing so each winter. We live in a climate where we sometimes reach extreme negative temperatures. Because adding supplemental heat to the coop can cause fires, it is important to only use them in extreme cases. We usually wait till we are well into the negative digits. It is also important to make sure the supplemental heat source is secured as safely as possible so that it is not knocked over by a fluttering flock.

Chores and Cleaning

Now that you have a coop set up, you will need to do some housekeeping. Some chores need to be done daily, while others are done once or twice a year depending on the number of chickens you have.

DAILY CHORES

- Open the pop door first thing in the morning to let your flock into their run or out to free range.

- Clean and fill food and water containers.

- Refill supplement bowls for oyster shells and grit.

- Check nest boxes for eggs and clean or refresh nesting materials if needed.

- Watch each member of the flock to make sure no one is ill or acting funny.

- Look around your coop for predator tracks, holes in fencing, or signs of digging.

- Spot clean any large messes, piles of poop, wet bedding, etc.

- Check for eggs again in the evening.

- Close and lock up the coop before dark.

WEEKLY CHORES

- Sanitize feeders and waterers and allow them to dry fully before refilling.

- If you use a run, you will want to rake up any poop and mess in the run.

- If you are using a mobile coop, relocate it to a fresh area of lawn.

- Scrap down dropping boards or shovel out coop floor litter.

AS NEEDED OR ONCE A YEAR CHORE

- Clean and sanitize your coop from top to bottom. Since we use the deep litter method of bedding, we do this in the spring and as needed till fall. Make sure to compost your chicken's poo and bedding as it makes great fertilizer for the garden!

7

Predators and Playtime

Sometimes it's the things we don't see that can cause the most problems. For chicken keepers, those unseen dangers are a wide variety of domestic and wild predators that would take any opportunity they can to steal away with one of your chickens. When it comes to the coop, secure doors and windows make all the difference. But what about when the chickens leave the coop?

When it comes to chickens spending time outside you can either provide them a run or let them free range. A run is an enclosed section of the yard where your chickens can scratch, dust bathe, and exercise. If you free range your flock, it means they are allowed to wander the yard in search of bugs, rest under bushes, and do whatever they want, wherever they want. There are pros and cons to each.

Keeping Chickens in a Run

If you plan to have a run, each chicken will need at least 10 square feet of space. While the chickens will have a door from the coop into the run, you should also have access so that you can go in to spend time with the flock and clean up the area. The run should be built out of sturdy lumber and hardware cloth or welded wire, NOT chicken wire. Chicken wire is not as strong as other fencing material and easier for predators to bend and break.

The smaller the gauge of wire you use, the better. Smaller gauge fencing is stronger and will keep out not only larger predators, but also predators like weasels or raccoons who may reach a hand through to grab one of the chickens. When building your run, make sure to keep in mind many predators can dig. When putting up the wire, it is best to dig a trench and bury a foot of the fence to discourage predators who might try to dig their way into the run.

A run will also need to be covered to protect against animals climbing up and in or flying in. You can use the same material you used for the walls or you can add plastic or metal roofing sheets. I recommend that a portion of the run have a solid roof so that your flock will be able to use the run in bad weather. In the winter, if you live in a cold climate, you can wrap your run in plastic to cut down on the wind.

While using a run does keep your flock safer from predators, there are some things to keep in mind. First, the grass in the run will disappear over time. Chickens can be rough on vegetation with all their scratching and poop. Second, you will have to make sure they have everything they need, like a dust bathing area, different levels to encourage them to exercise, and items to keep them busy so that there is no bullying. Check out chapter 12 for boredom busting ideas for your flock!

Letting Chickens Free Range

Because your flock will be able to wander around in the open, predators can be more of an issue. It is important that you have areas of cover for the flock to use in case they need to hide or make an escape. We have lots of plants and bushes around our yard for our flock to use as shade in the summer, but they also serve as hiding spots from predators. Being prey animals, chickens sense danger and will try to avoid it. Having a raspberry patch to dive into or a large bush to duck under in case they need it is important.

Because our chickens can wander a wider area in their search for bugs, they do less damage to our yard. We don't have to provide a designated dust bath area because they will find their own perfect spot for this activity. We don't have to build areas for them to exercise or provide activities to keep them from being bored, but it is still fun to do so. Flocks that free range can get away from each other and don't seems to get on each other's nerves as much as a flock that is kept in a run.

We also get to spend more time interacting with our flock. We don't have to go into a run to spend time with them because they meet us at the back door when we go out. They enjoy following us around and hanging out while we BBQ or garden. While we enjoy this, it may not be for everyone. Our chickens sit in our lawn chairs and sometimes poop on them. When we eat outside, they beg worse than our dog and have been known to hop up to the table and try to steal a pork rib every once in a while. While we find this entertaining, your family may not.

Be aware that if you have flower beds or a garden, your chickens will not respect these areas. We have had to fence in our garden and I have had to accept them dustbathing in my flower beds and nibbling my hostas. But it is a small price to pay for amazing eggs and great friendship.

For us, we find that even with the possibility of predators, our chickens have healthier and happier lives by being able to go about their business. We of course do everything we can to help make sure predators aren't a problem, but we are fully aware they can be. If you free range your flock, you will still need to make sure they are locked up safe and sound in their coop every night.

Common Predators

From stray cats and domestic dogs to raccoons and hawks, there is a whole cast of critters who would love nothing better than to get ahold of your chickens. So, what is a chicken keeper to do? The best answer for protecting your flock is preventing predators from getting to it. Of course, this is sometimes easier said than done.

With the loss of their natural habitat, more wild animals are entering urban settings. Just because you have never seen a coyote or hawk doesn't mean they aren't around. Take the time to get to know what kinds of wildlife live in your area. Coyotes, foxes, raccoons, weasels, skunks, opossums, snakes, hawks, and owls are just a few of the more common animals that would love to make a snack out of your chickens.

Let's take a closer look at some of these predators.

Dogs and Coyotes

Dogs that are allowed to run free can be a problem for your flocks. They sometimes kill simply for the fun of it, while some would not act on these instincts. Dogs are descended from wolves and still have some of the hunting instinct of their ancestors. Keep in mind, not all dogs will attack a flock. In fact, some breeds are good guard dogs for your flock.

So, what makes a dog attack chickens? The breed of the dog may play a part, the presence of other dogs, and the dog's past experiences. Some breeds have a greater tendency to chase than others. This can be made worse if other dogs are nearby, because a pack mindset can be triggered. Also, if a dog has had success in the past at getting food by attacking chickens, it will likely repeat the behavior.

While dogs usually attack during the day, coyotes are primarily nocturnal. If your chicken is killed during the day it was most likely a dog. If you find a chicken killed overnight, it was probably a coyote.

Cats

Even well-fed domestic cats will kill young birds. Our cats, who never go out and always have food, are forever going after our parakeets. Cats will snatch chicks and smaller chickens but might think twice before going after a full-grown adult. If a small chick disappears or all you find are wings, it was probably a cat.

Bobcats

A bobcat is about twice the size of a typical domestic cat. Like cats, bobcats can see in low light. They prefer to hunt during dawn and dusk but can attack any time of day. Being larger than a domestic cat, they can easily carry off an adult chicken. While bobcats prefer woodlands, they will come into backyards in search of food. Don't think there are bobcats where you live? Think again! They are the most common wildcat in the United States.

Foxes

You may have heard the saying "like a fox in a hen house," meaning someone has bad intentions. That's because a fox in your hen house has only one thought on its mind and it's not a good one. Normally when a fox has been in the hen house, you will find a few drops of blood and feathers because the fox carries away the chicken. Most foxes live in wooded areas or on open plains, where they dig dens in the ground.

Raccoons

Garbage cans attract raccoons to urban areas. Once a raccoon finds food, it will tend to hang around, looking for other food, like your chickens. Raccoons take several birds at the same time because they tend to only eat the breast and crop area. Avoid leaving out cat or dog food for your pets, as it will attract raccoons.

Weasels

Weasels are long and slender, making it possible for them to get into areas through very small openings. They can squeeze through holes as small as ¼-inch in diameter! They don't weigh very much, usually less than a pound, making them hard to trap. They are active day and night year-round, but are rarely seen. We experienced a weasel attack on our flock and I was shocked because we had lived here 16 years and never seen one!

They are ravenous eaters and will kill multiple chickens at one time, and sometimes just for fun. Because they are so small, they kill larger prey by biting them at the base of the skull. The night we had a weasel get in, it killed three chickens and a duck, while injuring another duck too. Weasels are nasty little predators.

Skunks

Skunks love chicken eggs. They will open an egg at one end and lick out the contents. Skunks may remove eggs from the nest, but don't usually take them more than three feet away. While skunks don't kill many adult chickens, they will injure many in their attempt to get one.

Opossums

Opossums are omnivorous, which mean they eat a wide variety of plants and animals. When an opossum raids a coop, it usually kills only one bird at a time. Opossums usually begin feeding on adult poultry at the vent opening. They consume young poultry completely, typically leaving behind only a few feathers.

We have had issues with opossums from time to time wandering into our coop, but they have never harmed a chicken. They usually eat any chicken food they can find, or steal eggs. Since they eat ticks, we do not harm them, but rather work to relocate them back outside of the shed where they can resume being wild.

Hawks

The most common hawks that attack chickens are red-tailed, red-shouldered, and Cooper's hawks. Hawks typically attack during the day. They have very good eyesight and scan for prey from elevated perches. Hawks are usually patient hunters who watch and wait. A hawk can carry off a young or bantam chicken and eat it elsewhere, leaving no sign other than a missing chicken. If a hawk eats a chicken where it kills it, it will pluck the breast area before eating.

While many folks enjoy bringing songbirds to their yards by placing wild bird feeders, as a poultry keeper, it is an activity that can be harmful to your flock. Hawks enjoy grabbing a quick meal and bird feeders provide a smorgasbord of opportunity. As the number of wild birds increase, so will your hawk population.

Hawks migrate and you could see an increased number of them in spring and fall. Most hawks are soaring birds, which means they depend on updrafts to help them travel. Large bodies of water have no updrafts, so the raptors tend to follow the

shorelines in order to get around larger bodies of water. Chicken keepers around the Great Lakes, both coasts, and the Gulf of Mexico should be especially alert during hawk migration.

All hawks are federally protected under the Migratory Bird Treaty Act. Check with your local Department of Natural Resources before trying to deal with a hawk problem. In the state of Michigan, we were told we can't even turn a water hose on a hawk. The best you can do is to try to scare them off by putting mylar balloons around the coop, hanging reflective items such as old CDs, and playing loud music, which your neighbors might not like.

Red-Tailed Hawk

The red-tailed hawk is one of three species sometimes referred to as chicken hawks. Red-tailed hawks live in a wide variety of habitats, including grasslands, farm fields, pastures, parks, and woodlands. They need an open hunting area with several scattered perches to swoop down from.

Red-Shouldered Hawk

Though red-shouldered hawks usually eat rodents and other small mammals, they will eat poultry if the opportunity arises. Red-shouldered hawks live in forests and swamps.

Cooper's Hawk

Cooper's hawks, which can fly well through heavily wooded areas, prefer to live in deciduous and mixed forests.

Owls

Owls are more active at night, and that is when they typically take chickens. Great horned owls are usually responsible for attacking chickens. Barn owls don't normally bother with chickens. Great horned owls live in many types of habitats, from coastlines to grasslands to mixes of woods and open fields.

Owls are federally protected under the Migratory Bird Treaty Act. Check with your local Department of Natural Resources before trying to deal with an owl problem. Your best solution is to make sure to keep your flock inside from dusk till dawn.

Snakes

Snakes typically enter a coop in order to eat eggs. Rat snacks will also eat young chicks. Unlike skunks and opossums, who leave shells behind, snakes normally swallow them whole. Not all snakes are bad! Many snakes will hang out around a coop in order to feed on rodents like mice and rats who are trying to steal your chicken food. The only way you will know if you have an egg-eating snake is if you catch it in the act or the hole it came in through is too small for it to get back out after it has eaten the egg.

Many times, you find out a predator has visited after the damage is done. So how do you tell what has killed your chicken? It will depend on the clues left behind. While your first thought is sadness and wanting to clean up, you need to take time to figure out what happened.

If chicks are missing but there are no other signs, the offender may be a snake, rat, raccoon, or cat. They sometimes leave feathers and wings because they are not able to swallow them. If adult chickens are missing but there are no other signs, it is likely a dog, coyote, fox, bobcat, hawk, or an owl. These predators are able to kill, pick up, and carry off an adult chicken.

If you find a chicken missing its head, the predator is likely a raccoon. Raccoons sometimes pull a chicken's head through the wires of an enclosure and then can only eat the head, leaving most of the body behind. If the chicken is dead but not eaten, it is likely a weasel. As I said before, weasels like to kill for fun. Knowing how your chicken died will help you find the clues to who did it. Once you know who did it, you can take steps to make your chickens more secure.

Go tracking!

Mud and winter snow are great at capturing footprints of predators. Take time to look around your yard and coop area to see if you can spot any animal tracks other than your flock!

Dog

Coyote

Fox

Bobcat

House Cat

Raccoon

Skunk

Opossum

Weasel

8

What's for Dinner

When it comes to keeping any animal, you just want the best for them, and this includes their diet. Chickens need at least 38 dietary nutrients in the right amounts and balance. Thankfully you don't need to know them all because commercial feed companies have entire teams of poultry nutritionists that use very specific scientific calculations when they make up their food formulas. You will notice that there are different types of feed available depending on the age of your birds. These feeds also come in different consistencies including mash, crumbles, and pellets.

Many chicken keepers have a personal preference when it comes to the consistencies of the chicken food they use. We started out giving our flock crumbles only to find the wild birds liked the small size and would sneak into our coop. Our flock would also waste food trying to scratch at the crumble or accidentally knocking over their food bowl. We switched to the pellet variety in order to cut down on our food losses. You don't have to worry about the size difference between crumble and pellet, both standard size and bantam chickens can eat pellets just fine.

Chick Feed

Baby chickens require a lot of protein in their food because they grow superfast the first few months of their lives. When shopping for a starter feed for raising baby chickens, you will find "regular" and "medicated" feeds. The medication is a product called Amprolium, which is used to control coccidiosis in chicks. It isn't necessary to use medicated chick feed but it does help to prevent coccidiosis. If your chicks have been vaccinated against coccidiosis you will want to use the unmedicated feed. Chick feeds are a mash feed and have a consistency similar to sand.

Grower Feed

You can keep your chicks on starter feed for some time. Depending on whom you talk to, some chicken keepers suggest switching to a grower feed at around 10 weeks old. It has a slightly lower protein level but is formulated to sustain growth. When switching from starter to grower feed, your chicks may hesitate to eat the larger sized food. Let's face it, kids of all species can be picky eaters! You can transition them to larger food sizes by mixing the two feeds together so they get used to seeing it and they will be more likely to try it.

Layer Feed

Starting at around 18-20 weeks, you will want to switch your chickens to layer feed. This feed is designed to provide exactly what your hen needs to lay eggs. This feed contains around 16% protein and has increased levels of calcium, for proper shell development. Don't worry if your flock has a rooster, they can eat the layer feed too. It doesn't matter which consistency of feed you use because the nutritional value and cost will be similar. I don't recommend layer mash as it is easily wasted and can cause an impacted digestive system. Crumble tends to get wasted as well and will attract wild birds for a free meal. Don't worry, your chickens can eat pellets just fine!

How Much, How Often

Generally, chickens won't overeat. If you put too many pellets in their feeder, they simply won't eat them. If you find that when you lock them up for the night there is still food in their bowl, cut back how much you put out. You do not want to leave food sitting out at night as it can attract the predators we talked about in the previous chapter.

As for how often you should feed your chickens, that depends on your schedule. If you are away from your home during the day, it is best to feed them before your leave and check their food when you get home. If they run out of food regularly by the time you get home, try adding more food to the bowl in the morning. I feed our flock after I have driven my children to school, so our flock expects to be fed earlier in the morning because they are used to that schedule. They know when I am running late and give me an earful about it if I show up after 8:00 a.m.!

Calcium

Once your chickens have matured and begin producing eggs, there are a few dietary supplements you will want to provide for your flock, especially if you keep them in a run. Laying chicken

feed does contain calcium, but it may not be enough. Remember, each chicken is an individual, and some might need more calcium than others. It is a good idea to have a dish of calcium available to your flock. Do not mix it in their feed, just have a separate bowl available. The hens that need it will take it. Calcium can be found at feed stores in the form of crushed oyster shells.

You can also make your own calcium by feeding your eggshells back to your hens. As you use your eggs, simply rinse out the shells and let them dry. Once you have a cookie sheet full of shells, bake them at 200°F. for about an hour to kill off any lingering bacteria. Once the shells cool you can crush them up with a rolling pin. Making your own calcium is easy and free!

Grit

In order to properly digest their food, chickens need grit. Grit is coarse sand or tiny gravel bits that help grind up food in their digestive track. Chickens that free range tend to find their own grit, but chickens that are kept in a run will need you to provide a small dish at their feeding station. Grit can be bought from a feed store and comes in different sizes. Be sure to purchase the right size for the age of your birds.

Water

It is important to provide your flock with an adequate supply of fresh, clean water at all times. Chickens will drink three times as much water by weight as they eat in feed. Your chickens will drink more water during warm weather. During the winter if you live in a colder climate, the water will probably freeze. Be prepared to break the ice up and clean out the waterer. In extreme cold, you may have to do this a couple times a day.

While every book you read about chickens stresses how much they need fresh, clean water, be aware your chickens will drink from just about any water source they can find. I can't tell you how many times I have just finished giving our flock clean water, only to turn around and find them drinking out of a dirty puddle! Clean water is important, but don't worry if you see them drinking from puddles.

Good Treats vs. Bad Treats

You may be concerned about what brand of food you feed your chickens, but your chickens' diet goes beyond the bag. While some chickens seem to know what they should and shouldn't eat, others are little trash compactors, pecking anything (including Styrofoam) that they can get their beaks on. One of the many benefits of keeping chickens is that you can feed them a lot of different kitchen scraps. This means they get a varied diet and you get to save some money!

When it comes to what you shouldn't feed your chickens, you might hear other chicken keepers saying that some of these items are okay when they really aren't! Someone might say "But my Grandma used to feed her flock ..." or "I have fed my chickens XYZ with no problem," and maybe they have, but some of these items can be very toxic to your chickens. Toxins build up over time and effect each individual differently.

There is science to back the fact that dogs should not eat chocolate, right? Well the same goes for the following food items. There is scientific proof that by consuming once or due to a buildup of toxins over time, these foods can harm your feathered friends. So why risk it?

Foods That Should Be OFF Your Chicken's Menu

Onions contain a toxin called thiosulphate, which destroys red blood cells. Eating too much onion can cause vomiting, diarrhea, and other digestive problems in chickens. It has been found that prolonged exposure can lead to a blood condition called hemolytic anemia, which is followed by respiratory distress and eventual death.

Avocado contains the toxin persin. What does it do? Persin causes myocardial necrosis (aka, a weakening of the heart muscle). That means that over time your birds could develop cardiac distress and eventual heart failure. While there is a debate as to what part of the plant you can feed your chicken (no skins or pits), why risk any amount of persin?! Better safe than sorry.

Potatoes contain solanine, which can be toxic to birds. Solanine effects the gastrointestinal tract, causing diarrhea and cramps. Cooking the potato does not eliminate the toxin. Some folks say not to feed the "green" part of the potato, but the depth that the green penetrates is not always visible to the human eye. Sweet potatoes are fine as they are not in the same plant family as other potatoes.

Raw dried beans contain a toxin called hemaglutin. Symptoms of hemaglutin poisoning are diarrhea and vomiting. Yes, your chicken can throw up. To avoid exposure, make sure to thoroughly cook any beans that you choose to share with your birds.

Rhubarb contains high amounts of oxalic acid which can kill your flock. No part of the rhubarb plant should be fed to chickens.

Chocolate contains the toxin methylxanthines theobromine. What starts as diarrhea can quickly turn into a central nervous system issue causing seizures, as well as cardiac issues, which can both lead to death. Keep the chocolate for yourself!

Apples (along with cherries, peaches, apricots, and pears) contain trace amounts of cyanide within their seeds. While the fruit is fine for your bird, make sure that cores and seeds are not available to them.

Dairy products can give chickens diarrhea. Let's face it, chickens weren't meant to drink milk, thus they have no udders! If you do give dairy, such as yogurt, make it a rare thing.

Citrus can interfere with calcium absorption, which is extremely important for laying hens.

Uncooked rice can cause crop/digestive issues if too much is consumed and then swells up. Cooked rice is totally okay and, in fact, is one of our flock's favorite treats.

Coffee grounds have a small amount of caffeine left in them. Caffeine is toxic and the grounds have no nutritional value.

Alcohol is something you should never give your chickens. While they do enjoy eating the spent grains used to make beer, they should never be given the finished product.

Remember, while these foods may not necessarily be fatal in small amounts, toxins can build up and cause damage to your bird's health, or worse, death to your chickens. Don't risk their health—it's always better to be safe than sorry!

Keep in mind, you should never give your flock moldy food. If you wouldn't eat it, don't give it to them. Avoid foods that are high in refined sugars and loaded with salt. Too much salt can kill a chicken by causing things like electrolyte imbalance or heart failure. Chickens are NOT vegetarians. They do enjoy eating meat, but make sure to trim the fat off first. Just like in humans, too many treats can make a hen fat and fat hens can have problems laying eggs.

So, What Can You Give Your Chickens as Treats

Giving treats to your chickens is a great way to earn their trust and get them to love you! Chicken treats are also very helpful for use in training your flock. As a rule of thumb, you should not give chickens more than 10% of their daily nutritional requirements in treats. The best time to give a snack is in the evening, after they have eaten the bulk of their daily nutrition needs.

The healthier your family eats, the healthier the kitchen scraps you will have to offer your flock. When it comes to treats, offer a wide variety and feed everything in moderation. Check out the list below to find the right treats for your chickens.

Veggies

Beans, such as green beans
Broccoli
Brussels sprouts
Cabbage
Carrots
Corn/Corn on the cob
Cucumbers
Garlic
Lettuce, preferably romaine as
    iceberg doesn't have much
    nutritional value
Peas
Pumpkins and squash
Radishes
Spinach, in moderation
Sweet potato
Tomatoes, fully ripe
Turnips
Zucchini

Fruits

Apples, not the core or seeds
Bananas
Berries, strawberries, blueberries,
    cranberries
Cherries
Grapes, cut up
Melons, watermelon, cantaloupe,
    honeydew
Peaches
Pears
Plums
Raisins

Grains And Seeds

Oatmeal, raw or cooked
Pasta, cooked
Popcorn
Rice, cooked
Sunflower seeds

Proteins

Crickets
Earthworms
Eggs, scrambled or hard-boiled
Fish, cooked, no bones
Grubs
Mealworms
Meat scraps, including beef, pork,
    lamb, chicken, or turkey

Feed stores also carry scratch feed, cracked corn, and prepackaged treats you can give your flock. These are the equivalent of a chicken candy and should be fed sparingly. They can also be used to provide extra calories on a cold night and as rewards when training your flock.

The Great Oatmeal Debate

Chicken keepers have been giving their flocks hot oatmeal on cold winter days for over 100 years. Old timers swear by it as a good way for a flock to start the day when it's cold out. Recently however, some chicken keepers have begun saying that this isn't good for your flock. While it is not a complete or balanced source of nutrition, most "treats" aren't! So, should you feed your flock oatmeal as a treat from time to time?

Oatmeal contains essential B vitamins including thiamine, riboflavin, niacin, and choline. It also has copper, iron, magnesium, zinc, and calcium, which is important for laying hens. Scientific studies have proven that including oats in a chicken's diet reduces mortality, cannibalism, and feather pecking. And let's face it, chickens love it!

If you want to make this treat a more complete source of nutrition, add in fruit and mealworms!

To Ferment or Not to Ferment

Fermentation is nothing new. People have been using the process for food preservation for thousands of years. Foods such as sourdough bread, cheese, pickles, even beer and wine are all made by fermenting. Animal feeds can also be fermented! There are many nutritional benefits to using fermented feed and it can also save you money on your feed bill.

Fermentation is the process of creating probiotics and enzymes by allowing the feed to sit in water for several days. The feed begins to partially break down, making it more digestible for your chickens and improving gut health by introducing "good" bacteria. Because of the increased nutrients in fermented feed, your chickens will eat less, saving you money.

Fermenting is very easy to do. You will need a glass or BPA-free plastic container, dechlorinated water, and feed. If you have city water that has had chlorine added to it, you can make dechlorinated water by letting your tap water sit in an open jar for 24 hours so that the chlorine evaporates out. Scratch grains and cracked grains ferment better than pellets, but it is possible to ferment just pellets and crumble feed.

To ferment chicken food, add the amount of food you want to ferment to your container. You will then fill the container with your dechlorinated water so that the water covers the feed by an inch. Do not overfill the jar, as the food will swell as it ferments. Cover the jar with some cheesecloth and place it in a cool place away from direct sunlight.

You will want to gently stir the feed in the jar a couple times a day and make sure the water stays above the feed. You can always add more water if needed. You should start to see cloudy liquid and bubbles forming at the top. This is the fermentation process happening.

After three days, scoop out the solids to feed to your flock; you can reuse the liquid to start another batch. If you see any mold developing or the mixture starts to smell rancid, toss it out and start over. When feeding fermented food to your flock, only feed your chickens what they can eat in about 30 minutes to prevent it from getting moldy. Once you know how much your flock will go through in about half an hour, you can adjust how much you make each time.

The Scoop on Poop

Chickens are omnivores, meaning that, in addition to a commercial feed, they eat fruits, vegetables, and meat. We all know that what goes in, must come out. It's good to understand the digestive process and what the resulting poo can mean. Yes, poop is important not just for composting into fertilizer, but also for telling you about your chicken's health.

When a chicken eats, the food travels from the beak, down the throat, and into the crop. The crop stores the food before it goes into the stomach. Food can be stored in the crop for up to

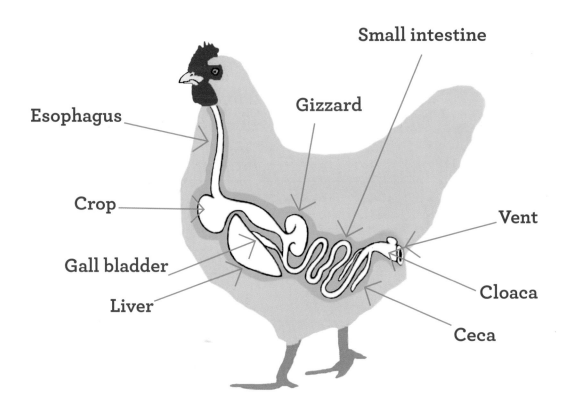

12 hours. Once in the stomach, the digestive enzymes and acid are added to the food before it all moves to the gizzard.

The gizzard is why chickens don't need teeth. It is a muscular part of the stomach and uses grit the chicken ingests to grind grains and fiber into smaller, more digestible pieces. From the gizzard, food goes into the small intestine. This is where nutrients are absorbed. The food that hasn't been absorbed then passes through the ceca. Bacteria in the ceca help break down undigested food. From the ceca, the food moves to the large intestine. This is where water is absorbed and the indigestible food dries out.

Chickens don't pee. Let that sink in a minute. Instead, the remaining "food" passes through the cloaca where the chicken's urine mixes with the waste. The urine is the white stuff on chicken poop. All of this stuff then comes out the chicken's vent as poop.

By looking at your chickens' poop, you can often get an early hint that something is wrong. Chicken poop is usually some shade of brown and fairly solid with a white cap on top. But keep in mind, what the chicken eats will cause the color of the poop to change!

While green poop could be the result of internal worms or Marek's disease, it is more likely that your chicken has been stuffing its beak with large amounts of weeds and grass. Yellow poop can be caused by internal worms or coccidiosis, or flowers. We have a forsythia bush our hens like to hide out under and in the spring, they enjoy eating the little yellow blossoms. And don't get me started on the rainbow of other colors I have seen come out of our hens due to red cabbage, raspberries, and other healthy treats!

You should worry if the poop is black. While they could have eaten something that caused the darker color, it can also mean they have blood in their stool. If you see blood, it's time to call a vet. More than likely you are dealing with coccidiosis. Runny poop can also be an indicator of health issues. It could also be that your chickens have been drinking a lot due to high temperatures or eating things high in water content, like watermelon.

Don't freak out if you find a giant chicken poop. These are usually from broody hens. When a hen decides to try to sit on eggs and hatch them, she won't get up a dozen times to go to the bathroom. Instead she holds it and waits. So, when she finally does do her business, it is BIG. Not to mention it smells pretty bad. But this is totally normal for a broody hen.

Normal chicken poop comes in all colors, shapes, and sizes. Usually there is nothing to worry about, as long as you can figure out what might have caused it.

9

All About Eggs

Your First Egg

Each chicken is an individual, just like people. It may seem like it takes forever to get your first egg, but it will come. It will depend on what breeds of chickens you have as to when you will see your first egg. Bantam breeds tend to lay earlier, while heavy breeds take longer. On average, hens start laying eggs at 20-24 weeks of age.

Once a hen starts laying, her reproductive system requires a few days to fully gear up. Her first eggs may be tiny and contain no yolk. The egg may be oddly shaped or have a soft, rubbery shell. This is because her body is still learning how to make eggs. Within a couple weeks, your hen will be laying normal sized and shaped eggs for her breed.

Egg production depends on nutrition, health, age, and time of year. After about eighteen months of laying, your hen will molt, or gradually drop her feathers, and she will grow a new coat of feathers. Most hens stop laying during the molt. The first egg laid after the molt may be small or otherwise odd as her body gets back in the swing of making eggs.

During the second year of laying, the hen's eggs will be bigger than before, but she won't lay quite as many as she did during the first year. Healthy hens will lay eggs regularly for the first two years of their lives. As a hen ages, her egg production will begin to drop. It is important to provide your hen with access to a calcium supplement. Do not mix it in with their food. Simply provide a container of oyster shells near their feeding area and they will eat as much or as little as they need. It is amazing how they "know" what they need.

If you have a small flock of laying hens you may be able to catch your hen in the act of laying an egg. Each hen lays an egg that is unique to her and you will be able to tell who laid which egg. In our flock, I know the brown eggs with speckles belong to Cinder. Large pale tan eggs belong to Buffy. Greenish blue eggs belong to Ester. When you know which hen laid which egg, it

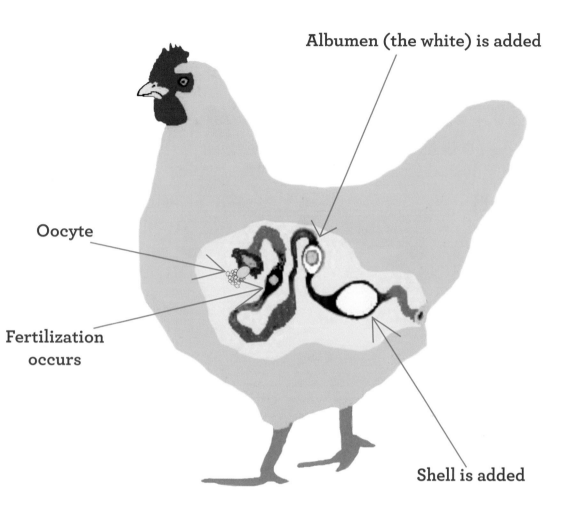

Albumen (the white) is added

Oocyte

Fertilization occurs

Shell is added

makes it easy to figure out who isn't laying, which could tip you off if there is a problem with their production.

Did You Know It Takes a Hen Approximately 26 Hours to Make an Egg

There's a lot that goes into the making of an egg and it's pretty amazing a hen can do it all in such a short time. An egg is made from the inside out. The yolk develops first, and is then wrapped in a layer of egg white, before being neatly packaged in a protective egg shell. Sounds simple, right? But it's not.

Your chicken's egg starts when the yolk forms during ovulation inside the hen's ovary. At this point in development, the yolk is called an oocyte. After the oocyte has fully formed, your hen's ovary releases it into the oviduct. If the hen has access to a rooster and has mated with him, the egg will be fertilized while it is in the oviduct.

The oviduct is more than 2 feet long. The forming egg rotates as it travels through the oviduct, developing the egg white, or albumen, around the yolk. The albumen consists of protein, water, and minerals. As the egg continues along the oviduct, it develops two connecting strands at the top and the bottom called chalazae. The chalazae help keep the yolk in the center of the finished egg.

The next stage is for the membranes to form around the albumen. It's kind of like putting it in its own Ziplock bag before the shell is formed. The membrane-enclosed egg enters the shell gland, where it spends the next twenty hours! The shell is made from calcium carbonate, the same material that makes up sidewalk chalk.

All egg shells start out white in color. Colored eggs have pigments deposited on them. Chickens that lay brown eggs for example, deposit the pigment protoporphyrin on the eggs late in the process of forming the shell. The pigment does not enter the inside of the egg, which is why brown eggs are still white on the inside!

Right before the egg is laid, it is enclosed in a fast-drying protein solution called the bloom, which seals the tiny pores in the shell. The bloom protects the egg from outside bacteria, allowing time for a hen to collect a large number of eggs in a nest to hatch.

Parts of an Egg

Yolk: The yellow part near the center.

Albumen: This is the clear part we call the egg white. It's called this because it turns white when cooked.

Chalaza: A thin strand that keeps the yolk in the middle of the egg and prevents it from sticking to the inside of the shell.

Membranes: Layers of film lining the eggshell that protect against bacteria.

Shell: The outer covering of the egg holding everything together.

Air Sac: This part helps regulate the pressure inside of an egg and also gives hatching chicks breathable air as they make their way out of the shell.

FUN FACT: A normal chicken's body temperature ranges from 105–107°F. That's why a freshly laid egg is warm to the touch!

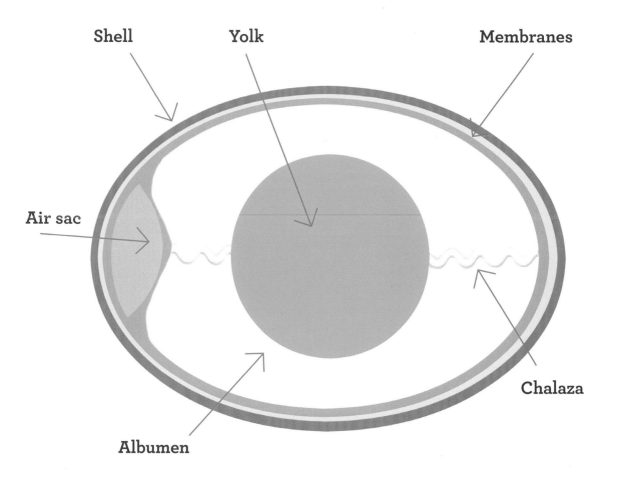

Shell   Yolk   Membranes

Air sac

Chalaza

Albumen

Collecting Eggs

Since your hens will lay eggs every day, you will need to collect eggs every day. In fact, you will want to collect eggs at least twice a day to help keep them clean and prevent chickens from eating the eggs. Yes, chickens enjoy eating eggs too. Eggs that get broken in the nest box become a tempting treat and can result in a hen that will break eggs open just to eat them.

You should collect eggs in the morning and in the evening. Allowing eggs to sit overnight in nest boxes often results in poop-stained or broken eggs. Not to mention it tempts predators who enjoy eggs to enter the coop.

Most hens tend to lay earlier in the day. You can listen for their "egg song," which is more of a loud cackling, sometimes bordering on screeching. To call it a song is being very generous. But why do hens sing an "egg song"? There are a few thoughts about why they do it. The first is that she is calling to the flock. Since hens tend to find a quiet spot away from the flock to lay their egg, this might be her attempt at finding them again. Some think it's to protect her egg. After laying she wanders away, "singing" to draw attention to herself instead of the egg. The last idea is that the hen is just so proud of herself for laying an egg that she wants to tell everyone.

You can use a pail or a basket to collect your eggs in. Of course, if you forget something to carry your beautiful eggs in, you can always use a coat pocket. Don't forget you have an egg in your pocket. There is nothing worse than a broken egg dripping in your pocket!

Cleaning Eggs

When an egg is laid, it has a bloom on it that seals the tiny pores in the shell. This bloom protects the egg from outside bacteria. You should avoid washing your eggs if you can so that you don't remove this protective coating. Instead, you should wipe the egg with a dry cloth.

If the eggs have a little dirt or poop on them, you can wipe small spots off with a damp cloth. A really dirty egg can be washed with a bottle brush. Always use warm water when washing eggs because cold water will make the egg shrink inside the shell and will draw in bacteria. If you do wash your eggs, let the eggs air-dry completely before putting them away.

There are a number of commercial cleaning products designed for use with eggs if you want to use them. These can be purchased online or at farm stores. You can also make your own cleaner by using distilled white vinegar. Simply mix together equal parts vinegar and water. Dip a paper towel into the solution, wipe off the eggs, and then throw away the paper towel.

Unwashed eggs will last at least two weeks unrefrigerated. Unwashed eggs will last three months or more in the refrigerator. Washed eggs will last at least two months in the refrigerator.

Storing Eggs

Did you know that in the UK, Ireland, and many European countries, eggs aren't refrigerated? Not even at the grocery store! Unwashed eggs can be left out for up to a month, though of course they will last much longer in the refrigerator. If you wash your eggs, they will need to go in the refrigerator right away as you have removed the protective bloom.

Eggs should always be stored with the small ends down. The air sac in the larger end of the egg helps keep moisture from being lost. Since eggshells are porous, they can absorb odors. If you are storing your eggs in the refrigerator you should use an egg carton or another covered container to cut down on the chance they will absorb the smell of other foods.

Eggs also freeze well. This is a great way to stockpile extra eggs during the summer to use when egg production drops in the winter. To freeze whole eggs, simply scramble each egg up and pour it into a muffin pan hole, then pop the pan in the freezer. You can also freeze whites and yolks separately. Simply separate the eggs and use an ice cube tray to freeze each yolk and white separately. You will need to add a pinch of salt to each yolk to keep them from becoming jellylike. Once your eggs are frozen, put them in a freezer-safe container or bag. Frozen eggs are good for six months to a year! When you are ready to use them, allow them to thaw in the refrigerator.

Is This Egg Good?

As eggs age, more and more air is able to get inside through the shell, allowing bacteria to get in. If you are unsure how old an egg is or if it is any good to eat, you can do a simple float test. Place the eggs in a bowl of water and watch what they do!

A fresh egg will lay on the bottom. An egg that is a few weeks old will start to rise up off the bottom, but it is still good to eat. An egg that is a couple months old will start to angle up or stand up

straight in the glass, but as long as one end is still touching the bottom, you can eat it.

If an egg floats completely off the bottom, it is very old and probably isn't safe to eat. The egg floats because too much air has gotten in through the shell. That means bacteria has probably gotten in the shell too. Toss any eggs that float!

Where Are My Eggs?

One of the great things about owning chickens are the amazing eggs they provide. There is nothing in the world like walking out to your coop and getting a freshly laid egg! But what happens if your nest box is empty? You might be asking, "Why aren't my chickens laying?!"

If you're new to owning chickens and bought chicks to start your flock, the first and most simple answer is, your chickens just aren't old enough yet. Most, but not all breeds will begin to lay anywhere from 16–24 weeks of age. New layers aren't always dependable and can go a couple days in between laying eggs.

Another reason you may not be getting eggs is that your hens aren't using the nest box! If you know your chickens are laying and you haven't seen any in the nest box for a few days, it might be time to go looking for that secret nesting spot. If you free range your flock, you will have to check around your yard too.

If you know your hens are laying and they haven't hidden their nest, then why aren't you getting eggs?

Molting: Most chickens molt (the process of replacing old feathers with new ones) in the fall. While some chickens go through their molt without much notice, others explode like a pillow fight went down in your yard! Growing new feathers takes a lot of calcium and so hens stop laying during this time in order to divert the calcium to growing new feathers.

Winter: Chickens naturally slow down egg production in the winter, it's normal. The decrease in daylight causes chicken to lay less. Heck, some hens may stop laying altogether. It is the natural cycle for their bodies. Commercial egg farms provide artificial light during the winter months to keep egg production up. Since it is a natural part of a hen's cycle to slow down and conserve energy during the winter months, we do not provide supplemental light to our hens. The decision to supplement light is up to you.

Weather: Extreme changes in the weather can play a role in decreased egg production. In extremely hot weather, you may notice your chickens panting. That is stress. Make sure you provide your birds with cool water during these heat waves. Similarly, an extreme cold snap can cause similar stresses on your flock.

Stress: We already talked about weather-related stress, but chickens can also be touchy. Simply adding new members to the flock may be enough for more sensitive birds to stop laying. Relocating to a new coop, even if it is still in the same area as their old one, can cause stress. If predators are bothering your flock, they could stop laying.

Broodiness: When a hen decides she wants to hatch eggs, she will stop laying eggs when she has the amount of eggs under her she feels is right. Yes, even when there is no rooster around, some hens will try to go broody. How do you know your hen is broody? Even if you are collecting eggs out from under her, she will sit in the nest box, all day and all night, if you let her. She may become more aggressive when you try to remove eggs from under her. Some hens will puff up and "talk" about the indignity of you stealing her eggs. Others can get downright nasty and start pecking the hand that feeds them!

Illness: Hens may stop laying eggs when they are ill. Chickens are really good at hiding their illnesses though. Many times, you will not know your bird is ill till they are VERY ill. That is why it is a good idea to spend time with your flock. Get to know their personalities and behaviors, that way you can tell if something is "off."

Age: Most hens lay well for about the first two years of their lives. By well, I mean steady and reliable. After about two years of age, a hen's productivity will decrease.

Predators: Sometimes wild animals will sneak into your coop and steal eggs. Look around for shells.

There are many reasons why your nest box is empty. Understanding the simple rhythms of a hen's life, from weather to age, can help you understand what is going on. And remember, it takes a lot of work to make an egg every day! Keep that in mind the next time you collect your eggs and make sure you thank your hens.

Egg Issues

The joy of raising chickens is that your eggs are always fresh. The egg making process is a complex one and sometimes things can get wonky. Commercial egg farms have these issues too, but they have a quality control department that only sends "perfect" eggs to the store, so you may be surprised when your hens have a "misfire." Normally an odd egg is just a one-time glitch and nothing to worry about. Egg shells take 20 hours for a hen to make. It is no surprise that sometimes this process has a hiccup or two!

Misshaped eggs: Sometimes an egg is longer and narrower or rounder than normal. While it looks weird, there is nothing wrong with the egg and it is perfectly edible.

Bumpy eggs: Bumps on an egg are just extra calcium. They can be small or large and can be spread all over the egg or just in one area. The extra calcium on the egg's shell does not affect the egg inside and it is perfectly edible.

Spotted eggs: As an egg travels down the oviduct, it spins. If it spins too slow, it can end up being speckled because the pigment isn't put on evenly. Some breeds, like the Welsummer, lay speckled eggs regularly. Just because the "paint" on the shell looks odd, it is still perfectly edible.

Soft-shelled eggs:
These eggs have a
VERY thin layer of
calcium instead of
a thick shell. These
eggs are usually
laid by newer hens
whose bodies are still
getting used to laying.
They can also be a
result of stress, lack of

calcium, and old age. Because they lack the thick protective shell,
bacteria can easily get into these eggs. Do not eat these eggs.

Rubber eggs: These eggs have NO shell. The egg is laid with
just the membrane holding it all together. The first time you
see one it can be a little bit of a shock. These eggs are also kind
of cool to touch because they are squishy. Just like soft-shelled
eggs, they can be caused by being a new layer, stress, lack of
calcium, and old age. Since the protective shell is missing, do
not eat these eggs.

Double yolker: Double yolks happen when the hen's body
releases two yolks into the oviduct at the same time. The hen's
body treats them as one egg and includes both yolks in a
single shell. Double yolk eggs are usually larger, which can be
a problem if it's too large for your hen to pass. If the egg is too

large it could cause the hen to become egg bound or suffer a vent prolapse. Double yolkers are perfectly edible.

Egg in an egg: This happens when a hen releases a second egg into the oviduct before the first egg has finished the laying process. This causes the first egg to reverse in the oviduct. The first egg, along with the insides of the second egg are all wrapped in the second shell and then laid. An egg in an egg is called a counter-peristalsis contraction. It's not common, but it does happen. I've never had one, but I have read they are still edible.

Fairy eggs: These are itty bitty eggs and are most likely the result of hormonal issues as a hen gets older. These cute little eggs are also called dwarf, witch, cock, and fart eggs. I like to call them "fairy eggs," which can be a lot more magical for kids.

In the middle ages, these fairy eggs were referred to as cock eggs. Since the egg contains no yolk it would not hatch, so some folks thought it must be laid by a rooster. A rooster is also referred to as a cock. In folk tradition, these eggs were thought to have wicked and magical powers. The superstition was that if allowed to hatch, it would produce a cockatrice (fearsome serpent) that would kill with its evil stare. To stop this from happening, you had to throw the egg over your house to destroy it, without hitting your roof.

Fairy eggs may or may not have a yolk in them. Instead of trying to eat something so small, we wash them and allow them to dry out and keep them. These are fun to show your friends.

Lash eggs or Salpingitis:

A lash egg is not an egg at all. These "eggs" are a sign that something is wrong in the reproductive tract of your hen. Lash eggs are pretty gross and are the result of an infection. Luckily these "eggs" are pretty rare. I have only ever seen one and I have raised chickens for over 30 years. Our vet had never seen one and was excited to get ours for her specimen collection.

A lash egg is made up of layers of all the yucky stuff from the infection. A lash egg can be soft or hard. It can be just a small amount of pus-like material or it can resemble an egg. It might even include pieces of egg. Why so varied? Well, because the hen's body is trying to capture all that yuck in her reproductive tract and get it out. Her body bundles up whatever might be in there and she "lays it" in an attempt to rid her body of the infection.

Lash eggs are caused by bacteria, including Mycoplasma gallisepticum, E. coli, Salmonella, or Pasteurella multocida. If left untreated, your hen could die from the infection. There are antibiotics that can treat the infection but you have to get them from a vet. As with any illness, the hen may or may not ever lay another egg depending how long the infection has been present. *Do not eat these nasty things!*

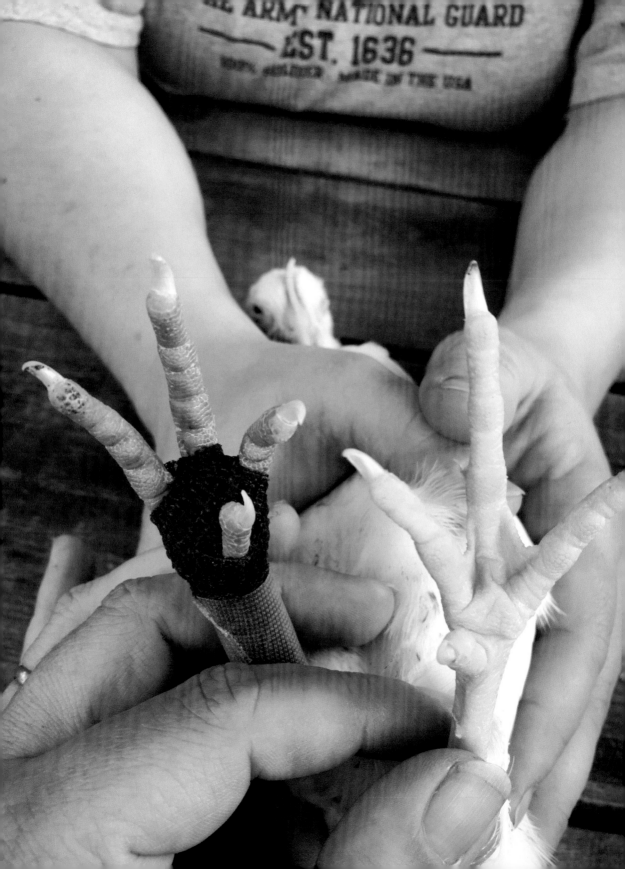

10

Is There a Doctor in the Coop?!

Chickens are generally healthy animals, but even the best loved bird can get sick or injured. Keeping your coop clean and providing quality food and clean water goes a long way in helping your flock stay healthy. Predator proofing is also important in avoiding injuries and death (see chapter 7).

Chickens are prey animals and try to hide their injuries and illnesses. This makes it hard sometimes to know something is wrong until it is very serious. It is important to check your flock every day. Make sure that each chicken is up, moving around, eating and drinking, and making well-formed poop. By spending time with your flock, you will get to know each bird's personality. By knowing how your chickens normally behave, you will hopefully be able to tell if something is off.

Keep in mind, most small veterinarians don't see farm animals or aren't familiar with poultry. It is important to find a qualified veterinarian BEFORE you need one. Our veterinarian will see our flock members in emergency cases but we are always charged an exotic animal visit fee. There is no need to worry because you can usually treat minor injuries and illnesses at home.

How can you tell if your chicken is sick? A chicken that isn't feeling well will act lethargic or sleepy. They may puff up their feathers even though it isn't cold outside. Other things to look for are coughing, watery eyes, and diarrhea. Sick chickens may stop eating and drinking, too. If you think your chicken is sick or injured it is best to separate them immediately in case it is something more serious and contagious. A pet carrier makes a great hospital room. The carrier needs to be kept away from the coop and areas that the other chickens might visit.

How to Do a "Cuddle" Check

It is good to physically examine your chickens from time to time to make sure they are in good health. If they are sick, you can use this same exam to find clues as to what is going on. Start off by holding or cuddling your chicken. If you do these exams often, your chicken will get used to the process and be less stressed out if you should have to do one because they are sick.

To properly hold an adult chicken, you want to start by facing each other. Slip your hand, palm up, under the chicken so that the majority of the chicken's weight will rest in your

palm and three middle fingers, while your thumb and pinkie
fingers go to the outside of the bird's legs to hold them still. You
can then tuck the chicken's head under your arm, like a football,
to carry them. You want them facing you so that when you lift
and carry, the vent is away from you. This helps cut down on
getting pooped on!

Start your exam at the chicken's head. The comb should be
bright red, slightly warm, and free of scabs. Check for swelling
of the comb, wattles, eyelids, and face. Look at the chicken's
eyes to see if they are cloudy or goopy. A chicken's pupil should
be round and the iris should be copper-red in adult birds and

blue-gray in young birds. Check the chicken's nostrils to see if they are crusty or runny. Check the beak area for any discharge or injuries. Open the beak to check for ulcers and lesions. The upper and lower beaks should meet at the tips.

Next you will want to check the chicken's overall body condition. Place the palm of your hand over the chicken's chest so you can feel the keel or breastbone. The keel sticks out from the bird's chest and is surrounded on each side by the breast muscles. Feeling this area will help you determine whether the chicken is thin or fat. If a chicken is in good health, you will be able to feel the keel but it shouldn't be poky. The breast muscles will be rounded and full but not so full as to hide the keel.

The next step in the exam is to check the chicken's feathers and skin. Lift the feathers to look at the chicken's skin. Look for lumps, scabs, and bruises. The color of a bruise can tell you the age of the injury. A fresh bruise will be red. A bruise changes from red to purple, to green, and then to yellow, as it heals. A yellow bruise can be up to five days old. Look for parasites like mites and lice. Do you see any scurrying specks or walking dandruff? Are there white clumps on the feather shafts?

Next you are going to check each wing. The chicken shouldn't mind too much having their wings extended. If your chicken begins to struggle when you extend a wing, it could be a sign of pain. Look at both wings before moving down to the legs and feet. The scales on your chicken's legs should be smooth. Rough leg scales can be a sign of mites. Check the bottoms of both feet looking for scabs, sores, or swelling.

The last areas you are going to check are the abdomen or belly and the vent area. Your chicken shouldn't mind you gently feeling their abdomen, unless they are in pain. If your chicken has diarrhea, then the feathers around the vent area will be dirty with pasty white or yellow poo.

Once you have finished your "cuddle" check, it is always nice to reward your chicken with a treat. A treat after the exam teaches the chicken that letting you handle them is a good thing. This is called positive reinforcement and it is how zoos train their animals.

What is Biosecurity?

Biosecurity is a set of preventive measures designed to reduce the risk of transmission of infectious diseases. Basically, it is using common sense to protect your chickens from getting sick.

What type of biosecurity measures can you take? Your shoes and clothes can carry diseases home to your flock. When you travel to other coops, or say a county fair, you bring home trace amounts of dirt or manure which could spread illness. Use a pair of shoes or boots that are strictly for using in your yard. I have a pair of shoes for going out in public and a pair for going out to the coop.

Ask visitors to your home who own chickens not to go around your flock. They too could be carrying diseases on their clothes and shoes. If you want to allow other chicken owners near your flock, have a washing and disinfectant station available. In one tub, mix water and dish soap for them to step in to wash their shoes. Next, they will need to step in a second tub of disinfectant that can be bought at a farm store. You can also make your own disinfectant with 1 part bleach to 3 parts water. After the footbaths have been used, dispose of the water away from areas your chickens go in.

Don't borrow poultry supplies, such as cages, from another keeper without properly sanitizing them before bringing them home. Many viruses and bacteria can travel on equipment. They can also travel on your car tires. Make sure to park your cars where your chickens don't have access to them.

Adding new birds to your flock without quarantine (isolation) measures is a huge risk. All new chickens should be kept in separate housing, away from the main flock for 30 days. This will give you time to notice any health issue they might have before they have a chance to pass it on to your flock.

Putting Together a First Aid Kit

Chickens are pretty hardy birds, but as a responsible animal owner it is always good to be prepared. You never know when two chickens will get into a fight, a predator will attack, or an unexpected illness will happen. Time is of the essence when it comes to caring for your chickens. Having supplies ready to treat these issues can make all the difference in keeping your bird alive.

The first thing you want to have handy is a place where you can isolate a sick or injured chicken. A "hospital room" can be a dog crate set up in your basement or a pet carrier you can place

CHICKEN FIRST AID KIT SUPPLIES

Adhesive bandage

Blu-Kote antiseptic spray

Cornstarch

Dawn dish detergent

Digital Scale

Disposable gloves

Epsom salts

Flashlight

Food grade diatomaceous
earth

Gauze

Liquid calcium or Tums

Medical tape

Nail file

Non-coated aspirin

Old clean towels

Pen/notepad to jot things
down in an emergency

Phone number of local
veterinarians who see
chickens

Poultry
Nutri-Drench

Poultry VetRx

Popsicle sticks

Preparation H

Probiotic powder

Q-Tips to clean injuries

Small plastic wash basin

Rubbing alcohol/hydrogen
peroxide

Rubber bands

Saline solution

Scissors

Syringe

Triple antibiotic ointment

Tweezers

Vaseline

Vitamins and electrolytes

in your bathroom. Next you will need a plastic bin to store all your supplies in. Having all your supplies in an easy-to-grab bin will save time and frustration when an emergency happens.

Diseases and Illnesses

Avian Flu

Avian Influenza is most commonly known as the bird flu. When an infected bird comes into contact with healthy birds, the virus spreads quickly. The movement of infected birds, or equipment used in the poultry industry, are factors in spreading the virus. The virus can travel on manure, egg flats, crates, and other farming equipment as well as on clothing, shoes, and hands of people who have been exposed to the virus.

Symptoms of avian flu include lack of energy and appetite, decreased egg production, and swelling of the head, comb and wattles, and eyelids. The comb and wattles, along with the chicken's legs, will develop a purple discoloration. The chicken might have a runny nose, coughing, and sneezing, as well as diarrhea and difficulty walking.

Unfortunately, there is no vaccine and infected chickens will always be carriers. Once your birds get this disease, they need to be put down and the body destroyed. You will need to sanitize any area that the birds were in before starting a new flock.

While the United States Department of Agriculture has identified the disease in wild birds and a few backyard flocks, the majority of cases of avian flu have been in commercial poultry flocks. If you are worried about the disease, don't allow visitors who own poultry to visit with your flock, because you don't know what they could be tracking in on their shoes. Don't borrow equipment from other poultry keepers, such as pens. If you are buying birds, buy only from folks you know and make sure to quarantine the new birds away from your existing flock.

Botulism

Botulism is a serious disease caused by bacteria from rotten meat that contaminates food and water. Symptoms include tremors that quickly progress to paralysis, including being unable to breath. Another symptom is a bird's feathers will pull out easily. Death can occur within hours of becoming sick.

This disease is avoidable by keeping your chickens in a clean environment and cleaning up any dead animals, such as wild birds and squirrels, from around your yard. There is an antitoxin available from your veterinarian, but it is expensive. If diagnosed early enough, you can try 1 teaspoon of Epsom salts dissolved in 1 ounce of water, given orally several times a day. You can use a syringe to give the mixture to your chicken by holding open their beak and injecting it down the throat.

Bumblefoot

Bumblefoot is an infection caused by the *staphylococcus* bacteria. A chicken can get bumblefoot by accidentally scratching, cutting, or injuring its foot. If the injury gets infected, the chicken's foot (and possibly its leg) will begin to swell. This is a very painful infection. When dealing with bumblefoot, wear disposable gloves because staphylococcus can cause infections in humans too.

Bumblefoot can happen very easily and there isn't much you can do to prevent it other than keeping your coop clean and free of debris that could cause injury. If you notice a chicken with a foot injury, be sure to wash and disinfect it to prevent an infection from starting.

A chicken with bumblefoot will not want to walk on the injured leg and foot. You may see the chicken holding the foot up off the ground or sitting often to keep its weight off the painful foot. When you look at the bottom of the foot, you will see a sore or abscess. There are stages to this infection. When caught early you will see redness or swelling of the foot and it may feel hot to the touch. More advanced infections have a black scab and a "kernel."

To treat bumblefoot and remove the infected kernel without surgery, fill a basin with warm water and Epsom salts and soak the infected foot for 10 minutes. Soaking the foot helps to loosen up the hard kernel from the skin. Using a gloved hand, gently work the skin around the kernel. Don't force the kernel out—you don't want it to bleed. If the kernel refuses to come out, be patient and soak the foot another 10 minutes and try again. Repeat this process till the kernel can be worked out of the foot.

Once the kernel is out, dry the foot completely and coat with an antibacterial product like Vetericyn. Cover the foot with gauze and wrap with medical wrap to secure the bandage and keep the wound clean. Change the bandage every few days and keep an eye out for symptoms of infection, like a bad smelling discharge from the wound.

Remember, staphylococcus can cause infections in humans too, so be sure to wear gloves and disinfect your work area with a bleach solution after you are done removing the kernel.

Coccidiosis

Coccidiosis (pronounced cock-sid-ee-oh-sis) is one of the most common chicken diseases. Symptoms of this disease include diarrhea that is bloody and/or contains mucus. Infected birds could also be weak, stop eating, have pale combs and wattles, have ruffled feathers, and act like they are cold when it's not cold. Coccidiosis is an intestinal disease that happens when a microscopic parasitic organism attaches itself to the intestinal lining of a chicken. In other words, tiny bacteria get in the chicken's tummy and do some really bad things.

This disease is usually seen in younger birds, like chicks in a brooder. The bacteria harm the gut, causing bleeding, and it stops the chicken from absorbing nutrients from its food. It's very bad news for chicks, who need a lot of nutrients to grow big and strong. It spreads quickly in young chicks because their immune system isn't developed yet. With coccidiosis, it is not uncommon for a chick to appear fine one day and very sick or even dead the next. This is another reason you should keep your brooder and coop clean and dry.

Coccidia multiply best in warm, wet, dirty conditions. It is nearly impossible to keep chickens away from these bacteria because they are everywhere, even in the dirt in your yard. Being exposed to it in small amounts helps your chickens build up an immunity to it. Chicks can be vaccinated against coccidiosis or you can use medicated feed as a preventative.

Coccidiosis is spread when an infected chicken poops. The parasites leave the chicken's body and can infect other bird in the flock. That's why it is important to quarantine (remove) sick birds from the flock. There is medication that can successfully treat this condition. The most common drug in treating coccidiosis in backyard settings is Amprolium. It can be mixed in the water and is used for 3–5 days for successful treatment. It is sold at most farm stores under brand names. Ask your store staff for help locating it. If you can't find it in a store, you may have to call a vet.

Coccidiosis wreaks havoc on the digestive tract, killing the good bacteria that lives there too. Once you have successfully treated your sick chicks, you can give them a little plain yogurt to help rebuild their gut health. While chickens don't process dairy products very well, the live cultures in the yogurt are valuable to intestinal health, so a little won't hurt them. You can also sprinkle a little probiotic powder in their feed to help rebuild the good bacteria.

Egg Bound

An egg-bound hen literally has an egg stuck in her oviduct. Being egg bound is a life-threatening situation, but not always a death sentence. Symptoms of being egg bound vary from bird to bird. Typical symptoms can include loss of appetite, being lethargic or appearing sleepy, drooping wings, frequent sitting, and abdominal straining (aka, their hind end is pumping but nothing is coming out). Some hens may pass large wet droppings, while others may not pass any droppings due to the egg blocking the vent.

Being egg bound usually happens in new layers or very old birds. New layers may experience being egg bound due to the size of the egg they are trying to pass. As a hen gets older, her pubic bones spread, thus allowing eggs to pass more freely. In fact, when a laying hen is being judged at a fair, the judge will award a hen with a larger pubic bone spread with a higher ranking. On average, a normal laying hen's public bone spread is two to three fingers across.

As a hen gets older, her eggs also get larger. An overly large egg can cause a hen to get bound. Obesity and poor diet can also play a role in a hen becoming bound. More than likely, being egg bound has to do with a lack of calcium. Calcium is not only important for the production of the egg itself, but for the muscles to be able to properly contract and move the egg through her reproductive system. That's why diet is so important.

As soon as you know you have an egg-bound hen, you must treat her quickly. An egg-bound hen will die if she is not able to pass the egg within 48 hours. Luckily, being egg bound is not all that common. Many online poultry sites recommend taking an egg-bound bird to a vet. While that is a nice idea, it isn't always possible. Many vets will not see "livestock" and those that do may charge you for an "exotic" animal visit. But fear not, you can help your hen along at home with some simple tips and advice.

First off, handle your hen with care. Do not squeeze her abdomen (her stomach) in an attempt to move the eggs. The last thing you want is for the egg to break inside, as this can cause an infection. Put your hen in a nice warm tub of water to help her relax. Sometimes that is all that is needed. A nice long soak and some private time in a dim, quiet place can be just the thing for the hen to relax and for the egg to come out. Repeat soaking in a warm tub every few hours till the egg comes out.

Other things you can do to help is to lubricate the vent opening with Vaseline or vegetable oil. This will help the egg slip out. You can also give the hen a calcium supplement to help the muscle contractions that are needed to move the egg out of the vent. You can buy calcium supplements at a farm store but in a pinch, you can grind up Tums or other human calcium supplements and mix them into some chicken feed.

As an absolute last resort, if you can see the egg, you can try to carefully extract the contents of the egg using a syringe and then gently crush the shell to remove it. This is very risky and your hen will most likely develop an infection. This must be your last resort, and you will need to visit a vet for antibiotics. I would suggest if you have to take this step, you ask your vet to perform the extraction.

As the saying goes, an ounce of prevention is worth a pound of cure. There are many things you can do for your flock to help avoid them becoming egg bound. You can start by feeding a good-quality layer feed. Diet is very important in laying hens. Next, you can offer crushed eggshells or oyster shell. Don't mix it in their food, just have it available so that hens who need it will go and eat it. Trust me, these birds are smart and know when they are missing something.

Just like humans, a healthy hen needs exercise. Our flock free ranges so they get plenty of running around throughout the day. If you keep your flock in a run, you will need to provide them with enrichments to help the ladies keep those abdominal muscles in top laying condition. Stumps of varying sizes to hop up and down on, obstacles they have to maneuver around, heck, some people even give their chickens swings to play on! Supervised free range time is another option you might want to consider.

Avoid supplemental lighting in your coop. A hen's body was designed to go through seasonal cycles and supplemental light really wreaks havoc on their bodies. Egg production SHOULD slow down in the winter months. While your egg supply might dwindle, it is nature's way of allowing lay hens to rebuild their depleted bodies in order to lay strong the following spring and summer. Supplemental light tricks a hen's body into continued egg production, thus draining her health further.

Feather Pecking

Chickens have a social order referred to as a pecking order. Mild pecking is normal in figuring out who stands where in the order. Feather pecking is much more aggressive, where one bird pecks or pulls out the feathers of another. Feather pecking damages the chicken's feathers, and can also cause injury to the bird's skin.

There are many reasons why one or more of your chickens may begin feather pecking, including overcrowding, boredom, stress, age differences in flock members, and protein deficiency. It is important to stop feather pecking as soon as it starts. Chickens are attracted to the color red, and any bleeding caused by feather pecking can cause flock members to attack even more.

Preventing feather pecking is much easier than trying to stop it once it starts. Make sure your flock has enough space, a good diet, and that you provide distractions, such as food treats spread around their living area.

Fowl Pox

This is a viral disease that is transmitted by mosquitoes, other chickens with fowl pox, and contaminated surfaces. Symptoms include white spots on skin and scabby sores on the combs. If you look in your chicken's mouth, you will see ulcers. An infected hen will also stop laying.

There is a vaccine available. If your chicken should contract fowl pox, good care will be important to their survival. Isolate the infected bird and provide them a warm, dry place to rest. You should give them soft food to help them keep their nutritional intake up without causing pain to the ulcers in the mouth.

With good care there is an excellent chance the chicken will recover. Birds who survive fowl pox will be immune to it and do not carry the disease. If you have a fowl pox outbreak it is important to clean daily, including scrubbing down waterers.

Frostbite

Just like humans, chickens can get frostbite. Frostbite is a serious condition and can affect the comb and wattles, as well as the feet of chickens. Prevention is always the best solution. Chickens can handle some pretty cold temperatures. Our flock has survived -37°F! What chickens *can't* handle is a draft. You can protect your flock by providing wind barriers, extra bedding on the coop floor, and having areas where your flock can get off the ground should they want to go outside. On extremely cold windy days it is best to keep your flock inside the coop.

The most vulnerable parts for chickens are the combs and wattles. White tips on combs and wattles indicate a mild case of frostbite. Worse cases of frostbite look like black areas on the tips of the comb and wattles. Black means the tissue is dead and will not grow back. Do not try to trim or rub off these black areas, as they are protecting healthy tissue underneath. Some chicken keepers rub their chickens' combs and wattles with Vaseline or Bag Balm as a coating against frostbite.

Chickens can also get frostbite on their feet. Frostbitten feet and toes will turn black—there may be some swelling and the chicken will have a hard time walking. If the frostbite is bad enough, those toes will either fall off or need to be amputated. Chickens can live with the loss of a toe, but might get bullied by other flock members. You can help prevent frostbitten feet by having roosting bars wide enough for your hens to perch so that their bodies completely cover their feet from above and the bar completely covers their feet from below.

Frostbite is usually caused by moisture rather than the cold temperatures themselves. That is why it is important that your coop has good ventilation to prevent a buildup of moisture. Recovery of the frostbitten tissue can take 4–6 weeks.

Heat Stress

Most chickens like temperatures up to 75°F. Once temperatures get up into the 80s and higher, a chicken's body begins to go through physical changes in order to deal with the heat. Chickens don't sweat, instead they regulate their body temperature through their wattles and combs.

When chickens start to become stressed by heat, you will notice a drop in how much food they eat, an increase in the amount of water they drink, and a decrease in egg production. Your first warning sign that the heat is getting to your birds is they will start panting, like a dog does.

Panting will help your birds cool off a bit, but it can also create some problems. While panting gets rid of heat by evaporating moisture from the lining of the respiratory tract, panting itself also generates body heat. Also, the loss of water in the respiratory tract can cause respiratory alkalosis. This is when a chicken expels too much carbon dioxide (CO_2) while it pants and its body fluids become more alkaline, causing the kidneys to expel unnecessary amounts of several electrolytes, throwing your chicken's system into chaos.

Another way chickens try to cool themselves is that they will hold their wings away from their body. This is a normal behavior, but it will let you know that they are becoming more stressed. At this point you need to monitor your birds closely, as no one wants to lose a bird to heat. The most important thing you can do is to be sure that they have access to cool, fresh water. You may need to refill the waterers a few times a day, changing them out with new cool water each time. You can also add ice cubes to the waterers to keep them cooler longer. Make sure the waterers are not located in the sun.

Another way to help your chickens beat the heat is to provide shade and to not disturb them when they are resting. The simple act of walking can increase their heart rate and place even more demands on their bodies. Our flock free ranges and we allow vegetation to grow along fence lines, which provides not only protection from predators from above, but shade during those long summer months. If you keep your chickens in a run, you can plant bushes in the run or place a tarp on part of the run to provide shade.

While your chickens' appetites will drop as the temperature goes up, there are plenty of ways to get them to eat that will help them cool off. Provide your chickens with fresh fruits and vegetables that are packed with water content, such as peas, tomatoes, grapes, cucumbers, and our flock's all-time favorite, watermelon. You don't have to give your birds a whole watermelon, they love the rinds just fine. You can freeze watermelon rinds during cooler temperatures just so you have them for your flock when they need them.

Another thing you can do for your flock is put a box fan in the coop to keep air circulating and provide a nice breeze. Some chicken keepers put frozen jugs of water in the coop as a form of air conditioning. We experience high humidity levels, so doing this in a confined space would just make the humidity even worse. If you do provide jugs of frozen water, do so outside. Trust me, if the birds want it, they will cuddle up to it.

If you notice a member of your flock succumbing to the heat, carry the chicken to a shady area. Do not take the bird into your air-conditioned house. The extreme change of temperature could send the bird into shock. Instead, place the bird's body in a cool (not cold) bucket of water. You want to gradually bring down the bird's core temperature. If you were to plunge an overheated bird in a bucket of ice water, it would send their body into shock and could kill them.

Once you get the bird's core temperature down and they begin to respond to you, getting them fluid is important. You can purchase electrolytes that can be added to their water. This is something you want to keep in your chicken first aid kit for emergency moments like this.

You might be a little nervous about your chickens' well-being during the summer after reading about heat stress. Relax! By monitoring your flock and providing for their needs, they should do just fine. When I see panting in the coop during the evening at lockup, I know it is time to get a fan going. When I see wings held out from their bodies, I know it is time to toss them some juicy treats. It is just a matter of being alert to your chickens' behaviors and needs.

Infectious Bronchitis

Infectious bronchitis is a virus that spreads rapidly. It is transmitted by contact with infected birds, contaminated equipment and clothing, and can travel through the air. Symptoms include gasping, coughing, and sneezing. The chicken may also have watery discharge from its nose and eyes. There is usually a drop in egg production, and those eggs that are laid may have soft, wrinkled, or nonexistent shells.

There are vaccines for infectious bronchitis, but because there are many strains, the vaccination doesn't always prevent the illness. Vaccination for this illness usually requires multiple treatments. Sometimes the vaccines can cause respiratory symptoms and illness.

Practice good biosecurity. Keep your coop and run clean and dry. Sanitize your equipment, shoes, etc. Quarantine any birds showing signs of respiratory infection. If your chicken

does become ill with infectious bronchitis, you should isolate
the infected bird immediately. Give sick chickens a warm, dry
place to recoup. Chickens that survive this virus usually recover
within 2–3 weeks. Survivors are carriers and can infect other
chickens for up to 5 months after the infection. You will need to
clean your coop and disinfect everything on a regular basis.

Lice and Mites

Lice and mites are tiny crawling external parasites that can
become a problem for your chickens if they are given the
opportunity to move into your coop and take up residence on
your flock. The difference between the two is that mites survive
by feeding on the blood of your chickens. Some mites live on the
chickens while others live in the coop, coming out at night to
feed. Lice do not feed on blood, they survive by feeding on the
skin scales and debris in feathers. They live their entire life on
the chicken.

Both are spread by bringing infected birds into your flock,
by wild birds and rodents, or by carrying them in on your shoes
or clothing. They are more widespread and active in warm
weather and during the summer, although some types do live
in cold climates as well. While their life cycle is only 5–7 days,
each mite can lay more than 100,000 eggs during that time, so
treatment must be repeated and ongoing to completely get rid
of them.

Mites and lice can be hard to see due to their size and color.
You should check around your chicken's vent and beneath the

wings, if you suspect these parasites. Infestations of mites or lice can cause feather loss, a drop in egg production, pale combs and wattles, anemia, and even death. You need to take action as soon as you've detected a problem.

Luckily, the types of lice and most types of mites that affect chickens do not infect humans. Remember to always quarantine new chickens and check them for any mites before introducing them to the flock. Make sure your chickens have an area for dust bathing, which helps prevent lice and mites. There are various treatments for these parasites, but many involve using chemicals.

Red Mites

Red mites are some of the most common mites that affect chickens, and one of the most annoying to deal with. Red mites live in your chicken coop, not on the chickens. The mites hide in dark spots during the day and come out at night to feed on your birds. Because these mites feed at night, you should treat your flock at night. You will also need to treat your coop. You will need to remove all bedding and scrub every inch of your coop. Once the coop has been washed down and dried out you will want to sprinkle diatomaceous earth (DE) everywhere. DE isn't toxic, but it will cause any remaining mites to dry out and die. Wear a set of gloves and dust mask when applying this much DE because it is a fine powder and you don't want to inhale that much dust.

Northern Fowl Mites

Northern fowl mites are similar to the red mite, in that they feed on your chickens. Unlike the red mite, the northern fowl spends its entire life on the chickens. This means that your chickens will suffer anemia much faster because the mites are always feeding on the chicken. You will want to treat your birds and coop as with other mites.

Scaly Leg Mites

Your chicken may have scaly leg mites if you notice the scales on their legs begin to lift up. This happens because the waste from the mites build up under the scales. This can be very painful for your chicken. You will want to gently wash your chicken's legs before applying DE to them. Some chicken keepers rub petroleum jelly over their flock's legs to cut off oxygen to the mites. You'll have to treat every two or three days for several weeks, and the scales may not return to normal. You will also need to give the coop a thorough cleaning. Follow the coop cleaning steps for red mites.

Lice

There are many different kinds of lice that like to make a home on your chicken. Each one seems to like a different part of the chicken's body, so lice can appear from head to tail. Poultry lice feed on feathers and poultry skin, so you don't have to worry about catching this type of lice because you don't have either.

If you think your chicken might have lice, check their vents, under their wings, on their breasts, and around the base of their feather shafts. Lice can range in color from clear yellow to dull brown and their eggs are laid in white clusters. Lice are small, ranging from a quarter of an inch to smaller. Just like with human lice, poultry lice spread from chicken to chicken through close contact. Poultry lice can also be introduced to your flock by infested equipment. Other signs of lice include feather loss, a drop in egg production, a fluffed-up, ragged appearance, and pale wattles and combs, indicating anemia.

Treatment Options for Lice and Mites

There are many different treatment options for lice and mites, and they are not created equal. Dog flea shampoo should never be used on chickens because it is toxic and not approved for use on chickens. While Sevin dust does effectively kill mites, it also kills nontarget insects, like the beneficial honeybee. Products made with pyrethrum only kill adult mites, not eggs. Ivermectin is usually limited to cases that don't respond to topical treatments or which present in an advanced state. You don't just use this stuff straight out of the gate. You should avoid eating eggs from chickens treated this way for seven days up to a month, depending on the source. Diatomaceous earth is a natural substance and is your best friends, sprinkle it everywhere!

While your chickens are suffering from mites, it is recommended you increase their iron intake to prevent anemia. Good sources of iron include:

Beet greens	Raisins
Broccoli	Scrambled or hard-boiled eggs
Collards	Spinach
Cornmeal	Strawberries
Dandelion greens	Sweet potatoes
Kale	Meat scraps
Molasses	Watermelon
Oatmeal	Wheat products

Marek's Disease

Marek's disease is a very contagious viral disease that is contracted by breathing shed skin cells or feather dust from other infected birds. Marek's is caused by a herpes virus which can survive for long periods of time in the environment. This disease is more common in younger chickens under 20 weeks of age. This disease causes tumors to grow inside and/or outside of the chicken. Symptoms include the iris turning gray and no longer responding to light. Chickens will also become paralyzed. Sadly, there is no treatment for this disease and it has a high death rate. If a chick does survive, it will be a carrier of the disease, meaning it can infect other birds. While there is a

Marek's vaccination offered by many hatcheries, it is not 100% effective.

Newcastle Disease

Newcastle disease is a highly contagious viral disease that is transmitted by infected chickens and wild birds. You can also carry it on your shoes and clothes. The symptoms include breathing difficulty, nasal discharge, cloudy eyes, a drop in egg production, paralysis of the legs and wings, and a twisted neck and head.

There is no treatment for this disease, but there is a vaccine available. Sadly, most unvaccinated chickens under 6 months old who contract the disease will die. The good news is that older birds usually will recover and they are not carriers afterward.

Pollorum

Pollorum is a viral disease that affects chicks and adult chickens differently. For chicks the symptoms include being inactive and difficulty breathing, along with white pasty poop. In adult chickens you will see sneezing and coughing, along with a drop in egg production.

This disease is passed through infected birds and by contaminated surfaces, like clothes and shoes. There is no vaccine available, but there is a blood test that can identify chickens who carry the disease. When buying chickens of any age, make sure you buy from a NPIP certified source. This means that the source flock has tested negative for pollorum and avian flu.

There is no treatment for pollorum. Birds that survive the disease will be carriers that will infect other birds. It is recommended that all chickens that get the disease should be humanely put down and the bodies destroyed so no other animals get the disease.

Sour and Impacted Crop

The crop is part of the esophagus (food pipe) where chickens store food before it moves down the digestive tract into the stomach. A normal crop can be the size of a golf ball or bigger, like a tennis ball, depending on the time of day and how much they have eaten. Sour crop and impacted crop are two different conditions but are often linked.

If your chicken's crop is hard, it could be impacted. This means the food inside is not moving through the digestive tract like it should. Since chickens digest as they sleep, the crop should be empty each morning. If your chicken's crop is not, it means that it is unable to empty properly. This could be caused by something they ate, like large pieces of food, long grasses, or things they shouldn't have put in their beak to begin with. It could also be from a lack of grit. Grit is what chickens use to grind up their food in their gizzard. Free range birds find their own, but if you keep your flock in a run it is best to provide it alongside their food.

If the crop becomes impacted, you will want to isolate the chicken and withhold solid food for 24 hours. Provide all the water they want. You can try to gently massage the crop with your fingers to break up the blockage. You may have to do this repeatedly throughout the day. In extreme cases, the crop may need to be emptied by a veterinarian who can go in and remove the blockage.

If your chicken's crop is squishy or you can hear gurgling when you press on it, and your chicken has foul-smelling breath, then the problem could be sour crop. This is a condition where the food in the crop ferments and a bacterial yeast infection occurs. This often occurs along with impacted crop because if the food isn't moving like it should, it will sit in the crop and ferment. Sour crop is not an easy thing to treat. You can try giving the chicken probiotics or plain yogurt, or adding apple cider vinegar to their drinking water. You will most likely need to contact a veterinarian for an antifungal medication to clear up the infection.

Vent Prolapse

A vent prolapse happens when a chicken pushes too hard and her insides come out her vent. When this happens you will notice soft, wet, pink or red tissue coming out the vent. This can happen due to infection, egg size, age, or a lack of calcium. A young hen trying to pass a very large egg can prolapse. Older hens who have lost muscle tone are also more likely to have a vent prolapse.

When our oldest hen prolapsed, I called our vet, who said there was little they could do beyond attempting to push it back in and giving her a stitch to keep it in. We decided to treat her ourselves. We started by giving the chicken's back end a warm bath. This loosened any stuck feces and cleaned the tissue. Once the hen was clean, it was time to get the insides back inside the chicken.

It helps to have two people to do this procedure, one to hold the chicken while the other uses a gloved finger to gentle work the insides back inside. Once the tissue is back inside the chance of infection drops greatly. Next apply Preparation H cream to the outside of the vent area. The cream will tighten the vent area up, allowing the chicken's body time to put everything back where it belongs. Preparation H also protects the tissue and relieves discomfort.

Once the hen is put back together, she should be placed in a dimly lit pet carrier. The dim light will help her from being stimulated to lay an egg. You should also limit food intake for 24 hours to cut down on bowel movements, but allow as much water as the hen wants. The hen's body needs time to rest and you don't want her straining to push anything out, which could cause another prolapse.

Worms

Chickens can play host to a variety of intestinal worms in their digestive tract. Common worms include roundworm, gapeworm, hairworms, and cecal worms. It can be hard to tell if your chickens have worms which is why prevention is so important. The symptoms for worms include diarrhea; weight loss; decreased egg laying; dull comb, wattles, and eyes; wanting to be alone; dehydration; and a loss of balance. Chickens with gapeworm will also stretch their neck gasping for air. If you suspect your chicken has worms, your veterinarian can test fecal (poop) samples.

There are two ways chickens become infected with worms, direct and indirect. Direct means the chicken eats the worm eggs when foraging. Indirect is when the chicken eats something, like an earthworm or slug, that is already infected with worms. To help prevent worms in your flock you will need to keep your coop area and run clean and dry. Worm eggs love wet, warm, mucky areas. There are also natural diet supplements you can offer your flock including food grade diatomaceous earth, apple cider vinegar, and raw pumpkin seeds.

Deworming chickens is a topic of debate for many chicken keepers. Some owners deworm their flock regularly with medication, while others prefer to focus on preventative measures. Deworming medication can be given every six months to a year. If you use medication to deworm your flock you will need to read the label carefully. Some dewormers have a withdrawal period for meat and eggs. That means you cannot eat any meat or eggs from your hens for the specified time the medication recommends. Many popular dewormers have not been approved for use in chickens or actually say not to use them on chickens that produce eggs for human consumption. It is up to you to read medication labels and make the best choice for your flock.

If you do have a chicken with worms that have been confirmed with a fecal test, you may have no choice but to use medication. Work with your veterinarian to find an appropriate medication and make sure you understand any withdrawal periods it may have.

Time to Call a Professional

There are many illnesses and injuries you can take care of at home. But sometimes you need to call your veterinarian. If you don't know what is wrong with your chicken, don't feel comfortable handling a problem, or your chicken hasn't improved with treatment after 24–48 hours, it's time to pick up a phone. Major injuries, like a predator attack that could require stitches, should be taken to a veterinarian right away. And sadly, sometimes you know a chicken isn't going to make it and is in pain, and your veterinarian can help end their suffering.

11

Behavior and Training

Like most animals, chickens prefer to be kept in groups. A group of chickens is called a flock. Watching a flock of chickens can be as entertaining as watching reality television. Chickens have very complex social lives and a wide range of interesting behaviors.

Chickens can recognize each other based on the shape of their combs, wattles, and heads. They can also recognize you! Research has shown that they can remember up to 100 individual chickens, humans, and other pets. They also have long-term memory. They can recognize another chicken that has been removed and returned to the flock, even after many months!

Another study showed that not only do chickens remember, but also they make choices based on things they remember. An example of this is when a rooster repeatedly tried to trick hens into approaching him by making a food call when he had no food. The hens realized that the rooster was being dishonest and over time stopped coming to his food calls.

In a study at the University of Bristol, UK, researchers did a study that showed chickens can think ahead and have self-control. The chickens were given access to two different keys to peck. One key would give them a little food, right away. The other key gave them more food, but they had to wait much longer for the food after pecking the key. It was found that the chickens were more likely to peck the key that took longer for the greater reward.

Common Chicken Behaviors

Vocalization

Did you know researchers have identified at least 24 and possibly up to 30 distinct chicken sounds? They can combine these noises to make up a kind of chicken language. There are distinct calls that let other flock members know

there are good treats. Hens "sing" an egg song after laying. Broody hens will growl and grumble when you try to take their eggs. Not only do chickens let each other know if there is a predator around; their different clucks tell whether it is in the air or on the ground! Allow yourself to sit and spend time with your birds. Watch your flock, listen to them vocalize, you might be amazed at what you learn about their language.

Communication

While chickens communicate through vocal calls, they also have other ways of communicating. Chickens use displays and changes in posture to let other members of the flock know how they are feeling or what they want. Communication plays an important part in the pecking order.

Pecking Order

If you intend to have more than a single chicken, you are going to need to know a little bit about the "pecking order" and how it works. The pecking order is a hierarchical pattern of behavior in a flock. In plain English it means there is a top bird, an alpha, who runs the show and all of the rest of the chickens fall in line under it, depending on rank within the flock.

The alpha chicken has first choice on food and water, dibs on the best treats, favorite nesting boxes, preferred dust bathing spots, and the highest roosting spots. Alpha chickens will maintain this control through clucks, stance, and the occasional peck. Other members of the flock will "make way" for the alpha. An alpha can either be a rooster, if your flock has one, or a dominant hen will fill the role if you don't.

If you have a rooster, and only one rooster, he will likely take the alpha role as he reaches maturity. If you have more than one rooster in your flock, the roosters will battle for dominance.

With enough space and hens available, multiple roosters will create their own mini flocks (the hens they watch over) within the larger flock and can coexist without too many squabbles.

In a flock composed entirely of hens, there will be one dominant female who will establish herself as the alpha in the absence of a rooster. Younger birds are typically lower in the hierarchy, and older or more aggressive birds will rise to the top. If you introduce a rooster to your flock later, the alpha hen may continue to hold rank. We had two roosters who our alpha hen, Goldie, not only put in their spot, but also kept them there till we rehomed them.

Believe it or not, the pecking order begins the moment chickens come out of their shells. As chickens age or members of the flock come and go, the social structure will change. The stronger (and pushier) birds will move up in rank while the more submissive will move down in rank. Maintaining the pecking order can sometimes appear rude to us as we watch our chickens peck at each other, but this is natural behavior in a flock. A balanced pecking order is necessary for the flock to function properly. When each bird knows where it stands, the flock will be content and live in harmony.

Since the pecking order changes over time, with the introduction of new birds or the loss of others, remember there will be squabbles. If a hen or rooster is sick or becomes injured, they will lose their place in the pecking order and will need to fight for it again once they recover. New birds will also have to assert themselves to gain ranking in the flock. Disputes can be minor and last only a few seconds with a peck or two, or they can turn downright nasty and end with serious injuries or even death. While the flock needs to figure the pecking order out themselves, you should step in if the pecking becomes too much. No one wants an injured bird!

To avoid serious injuries when introducing new chickens to your existing flock, it is best if they can see and hear each other, but can't physically interact. We put our new members, usually chicks, in an upside-down baby playpen; this way the older hens can see the babies but can't hurt them. This gives everyone the chance to start the pecking order process by getting acquainted without coming into contact with each other. As they size each other up, you can kind of get an idea of how they may act once they are together.

Everyone feels bad for the underdog, but in every group, there is a low man, someone who brings up the rear. It's just the way life is. You can help avoid conflict by providing multiple feed and water areas, plenty of roosts in the coop, and plenty of "hiding" places for lower ranking members to get away from or avoid more dominant flock members.

Remember, YOU are part of your flock and the pecking order! You do NOT want to be at the bottom of the hierarchy. Sometimes a rooster will try to challenge a human. If a rooster dances around you with its wings out and charges towards you, they are trying to dominate you. This is when you need to establish your dominance. Some roosters will peck and jump at you with their spurs and will attack you if you turn your back.

If you catch aggressive behavior early, you need to put a stop to it. Never run from the chicken, this only supports their view that they are dominant over you. You should stand your ground. If a chicken still tries to attack you, you can grab them and pin them down on the ground or pick them up and hold them till they calm down. You may have to do this a few times, but a smart bird will soon learn its place.

Sometimes you will find a chicken who will not give up on trying to dominate you. In that case you have limited choices. You can live with it, rehome it (make sure you tell the new owner it is aggressive), or send it to freezer camp. Understanding flock dynamics will give you a better insight into the "secret" lives of chickens. It will help you identify if your flock has needs, like more feeding stations or nest boxes.

Preening

Preening is the act of grooming. Just like you take a bath and comb your hair, chickens need to take care of their feathers. Feathers are very important for insulation and waterproofing. Feathers are composed of a shaft with barbs. These barbs are held together by smaller barbules. Sometimes the barbs are pulled apart and the feathers can't do their job properly.

Chickens have an oil gland near the base of the tail, called the preen gland. Chickens pinch this gland with their beaks to extract a waxy oil. The oil is put on the feathers as they pass the feathers through their beaks. This causes the barbs to go back together making the feathers better able to perform their intended functions. Chickens also need to keep their feathers oiled to prevent them from becoming brittle.

Dust Baths

First time chicken keepers may be a little startled the first time they see one of their birds in the act of dust bathing. Why? Because it can look like they are injured or having a seizure! A bird flopping around on the ground can be startling. Finding a chicken who has finished dust bathing, when they are relaxed and sleeping in a twisted manner, can cause your heart to jump as they may appear dead. Just ask my hubby who found a hen so blissed out after a dust bath he actually had to poke her to get her to wake up and move!

So, what is a dust bath and why do chickens do it? The "what" part is pretty simple, it is part of a chicken's preening regimen. Preening is a bird's way of grooming its feathers to keep them in the best condition. Preening involves a few components, including the dust bath!

The act of dust bathing is when a bird (yes, some wild birds do it too) finds a spot and begins by scraping their feet in dry dirt or sand to create a wallow. If your chickens free range, that spot will usually be in your garden or flower beds, because chickens just don't respect boundaries and there is usually plenty of dirt and dust in these areas. If you don't want your garden or flower beds to have flopping chickens in them, you will have to fence them off.

Once a chicken has loosened up the ground, they lay down and begin rolling. They will rock back and forth to create a depression. A favorite area that is used over and over will develop a deep depression and I sometimes wonder if they are trying to dig to China! Once in the depression, a chicken will flap their wings and flop around in order to spread the dust over their entire body. They will fluff up, tail spread, so they can get the dirt closer to their skin.

Dust bathing is a behavior chickens are born with, knowing it needs to be done and how to do it. From a very young age, chicks in a brooder will begin to try to dust bathe. They will use whatever is available, the wood shavings you are using as their bedding or even their feed! I said they knew they were supposed to do it, it just takes some time for them to figure out WHERE they should be doing it!

It is a good idea to provide your brooder babies with the opportunity to dust bathe. You can give them an area in the brooder or have a separate tote with sand in it they can use during "exercise time." It is so fun to watch chicks learning how to move their bodies just right to pull off a proper dust bath.

A dust bath can be a lot of work and many times after preforming the act, a chicken will take a nap right in the wallow! Do not be alarmed if you find a chicken all twisted, sleeping in the dirt, especially if it is a sunny day. The chicken's wings may even be spread out in an odd manner. It is okay, just chalk it up to a really exhausting but good dust bath!

So what purpose does dust bathing serve in the preening regimen of chickens? The dust that is worked into the bird's feathers will absorb extra oil to help keep the feathers in tip-top shape. The oil-soaked dust is easily shaken off, and let me tell you, watching a chicken shake after a dust bath is funny, like a little dirt explosion! Besides keeping the feathers clean, a dust bath also helps feathers be more effective with insulating. The process of dust bathing helps with the removal of dry skin and other debris a chicken may have. Regular dust baths can also help with mites and other parasites as well.

Our hens simply flop in all-natural dirt to take their dust baths, but some folks like to add things to a dust bathing area like wood ash and diatomaceous earth, both of which might help if you have an existing mite or parasite problem. Taking regular dust baths is an important part of a chicken's preening regimen, so make sure you provide them with access to what they need to do the job. Not only will your chickens feel good and look good, but watching them dust bathe is very entertaining!

Foraging

Foraging is about looking for food. Chickens will peck and scratch as they search for things to eat. Giving chickens a complete feed makes it so chickens don't need to forage to get all the nutrients they need, but they will still forage

even when food is available. Why? Why not! There is nothing more fun for a chicken then to find a plump grub or to snitch a juicy strawberry from the garden. Just because they have food available, doesn't stop them from looking for extra goodies.

Tidbitting

This is a form of communication that uses both vocal and visual cues to let other members of the flock know there is desirable food. Mother hens do this behavior with their chicks to teach them what to eat while out foraging. The hen will make a series of high-pitched clucks and will pick up and drop the food at her chicks' feet. Roosters also tidbit for hens they are trying to woo. They will make a cluck sound and drop the food at the hen's feet. Roosters also bob their head and hop from foot to foot.

Beak Rubbing

You may notice your chickens rubbing their beak on things and wonder why. More than likely they are just cleaning off food and oils from their beak. Chickens need to keep their beak in top condition and they may also be sharpening their beak or smoothing any rough spots, as a chicken's beak continues to grow throughout their lives. Some keepers even think it could also be a territorial behavior and that they may be marking their area.

Romance

Chickens have a simple courtship ritual, compared to some birds. The amount of "romancing" varies from rooster to rooster. Some roosters put on a show for the ladies, while others give a half-hearted performance.

When a rooster wants to impress a hen, he usually does a kind of tiptoe-like walk and struts around her a few times. If the hen is impressed, she will squat down as a sign of submission. The rooster will then stand on the hen's back. After they mate, the rooster will likely crow to show off.

Squat

Just because you don't have a rooster in your flock doesn't mean your hens won't squat. Squatting is a sign of being submissive. Your hens, once they start laying, will squat for a rooster or for you!

A hen may also be squatting because a squatting hen is a protected hen. By squatting and freezing in place when a predator approaches, the hen is very low to the ground and her vulnerable underbelly is protected. Also, predators, especially aerial predators, hunt partially by looking for movement, so by squatting and not moving the hen has a better chance at going undetected.

Nesting

Hens prefer to lay their eggs in nests that are in dimly lit, quiet areas. They will spend time using their beaks and feet to build a comfortable spot out of loose material that they can settle into.

Once a hen lays her eggs, she may stay in the nest for a little bit. It's a lot of work pushing out an egg every day!

It is important for pullets to have access to nesting boxes before they start to lay. Chickens are mimics, and the first layers or older hens will teach the remaining flock where to go when it is time to lay their eggs.

Broody

When it comes to raising chickens, sooner or later, you're going to get a broody one. As with all living things, there is an inner drive to reproduce, and chickens are no different. And when a hen decides she wants to raise some babies, it is known as "going broody."

What some hens don't understand though, is, well, you need a rooster to make babies come out of eggs. This is something our poor, sweet Cinder didn't quite get. You see, we have no rooster, but Cinder's desire for motherhood drove her to sit. By this I mean, she parked her overly fluffy bum on everyone's eggs and took over the nest box.

It is a sure sign of broodiness when you go to your coop and the same hen is in the nest box, morning, noon, and especially at night. While it could indicate other issues, like being egg bound, if there are eggs under her, it is probably because she is broody. A broody hen will pluck her own feathers from her chest to line her nest. Another good indicator is when you try to remove the hen from the box, she gives you an earful of chatter, sounding her displeasure at being ousted.

Every hen has a different temperament, so behavior can range from clucking to full-on attack mode. Yes, a broody hen will peck your hand sometimes. Other times they will give off warnings, such as raising their hackle (neck) feathers just like a dog does with the fur on its neck when it is upset. Even the sweetest, most docile hen can get an attitude when she becomes broody!

Most modern breeds have been bred for egg production, not for their broodiness. A lot of time and money has been spent over the years to breed the broodiness OUT of hens, because commercial chicken farms don't make money selling eggs if their hens don't lay because they are trying to sit on the eggs. You see a hen that wants to sit will collect a clutch of eggs over many days before she starts to incubate them by sitting on them. When she is ready to sit, she will stop laying. What commercial egg farmer wants his hen to stop laying every time she goes broody?

When a hen goes broody, she will sit day and night. She will eat and drink very little. If she is not sitting on fertile eggs that would hatch in 21 days, there would be no end to her sitting. It is very unhealthy to let a hen be broody when there is no end in sight to her sitting.

So, what do you do with a broody hen? Some folks suggest letting a hen sit till she gives up. While some hens will give up after a month, others will just keep sitting. This can be very bad for their health, because as I said, they eat and drink very little. Not to mention they are getting no exercise during this time.

You can always try to "break" a broody hen by trying things like removing the eggs from the nest box more often. You will also need to remove the hen from the box and put her outside with the rest of the flock. In the worse cases of broodiness, you may need to place a dog kennel outside of the coop with the hen in it. Do not put bedding in the kennel. Make her be outside! Make her be with the other members of your flock. Don't let her keep going back to the nest box. Put her in the coop at night, but a few days of forcing her to be out of the nest box during the day might cure her of her broodiness.

If you don't mind your hen going broody, you can always get some fertile eggs for her to sit on!

Molting

Does it look like a pillow just exploded in your coop? Does your hen look like a pin cushion? Relax, your flock is just molting! Molting? Yup, and it's a natural and vital part of being a happy, healthy chicken!

Chicken's feathers are made up of tiny barbs and barbules that grow off the feather shaft and lock together like Velcro to create a water-resistant and windproof coat. Under the protective outer feathers are the downy feathers that have more flexible barbs and barbules that allow the chicken to fluff and regulate heat.

Over time, the feathers get worn out and lose their ability to be preened back into shape. Kind of like your coat getting a hole in it. You can still wear it, but it doesn't do a very good job of keeping you warm and dry. While we can go to a store and buy a new coat, chickens have to go about growing their own. Molting is the process of losing the old worn feathers and growing a nice new set of protective feathers that will carry them through the colder winter months.

If you raise chickens from chicks, the first time they molt will be around 18 months of age. From that point on they will molt once a year, usually in late summer or early fall. Less sunlight due to shorter days is a natural signal to poultry that it is time to begin replacing their worn-out feathers. By molting in late summer and early autumn, chickens will be prepared for winter weather with a full set of new feathers to keep them protected from water, wind, and cold temperatures.

Sometimes a chicken will molt because they are stressed. Just like humans losing their hair, chickens will drop feathers if they are too overwhelmed. Stress can be due to severe weather, extreme lack of food and water, illness, moving to a new location, new members being added to the flock, being broody, predator attack, and the list goes on.

Generally, chickens take two to three months to complete a molt, but it can take more or less time depending on whether the chicken undergoes a "hard molt" or a "soft molt." A soft molt is where a chicken slowly loses feather over time, taking up to five months to change out all the feathers on their body. Most

chickens are soft molters. You will see a feather here and there from time to time, but for the most part, the soft molting process isn't that noticeable.

A "hard molt" on the other hand is where the chicken loses most of its feathers in a short time period. These are the chickens that basically explode everywhere and look naked. We have one hard molter and the first time she molted, I thought a predator had got her! There was a giant pile of feathers in the yard!

Feathers consist of 85% protein and growing new ones places great demands on a chicken's energy and nutrient stores. The biggest thing you can do to help your molting chickens is to increase the protein content of your feed or add extra protein treats.

Your egg production will drop during molting because a chicken's body needs a lot of resources in order to grow new feathers. Molting can be a little painful. Pinfeathers (new growth) are sensitive, so avoid handling molting birds if they seem to not like being touched. While molting can be dramatic for some chickens, there really is no need for alarm. Remember, chickens have evolved to be amazing little critters who know what to do, when they need to do it, and how to get through it with just a little love from us.

Roosting and Sleeping

At around three weeks of age chicks start trying to jump up to higher surfaces in order to perch or roost. A chicken's claws allow them to firmly grip what they are standing on while they perch. This ability keeps the chicken from falling off, even when sleeping. Chickens go to roost about half an hour before twilight.

When chickens sleep, they really sleep. If you ever need to catch a chicken, just go out after dark with a flashlight and you should have no problem picking them up off the roost. Since they are defenseless when they sleep, chickens prefer to roost as high off the ground as they can. Smart chickens also pick a spot that has overhead coverage to protect against bad weather and owls.

Chickens like to roost in the same spot every night. This is why you need to train your chickens to go into the coop at night. Once they are used to roosting in the coop, they will return

to it every night, making it easy to lock them up safely from
predators.

Chicken Dreams

We may not know exactly what chickens dream about, but we
do know they dream! Along with humans and other mammals,
chickens have a REM phase of sleep. This period of "rapid eye
movement" indicates dreaming. Maybe they are dreaming
about fat, juicy bugs, basking in the sun, or hanging out with
friends. Who knows!

Chickens have another phase of sleep that humans lack,
called USWS. Unihemispheric slow-wave sleep is when one half
of the brain is resting, while the other half is awake. This is why

chickens can be seen sleeping with one eye open and one eye closed. It is an evolutionary adaptation that allows them to keep watch for predators while they doze.

Chickens Have Feelings

Chickens are known to mourn when another chicken in the flock dies. They will show signs of depression if they are removed from the flock for an extended period and placed alone. This is something to watch out for with chickens who are ill and need to be isolated.

Chickens have also shown that they have empathy. In one British experiment, mother hens and their chicks were placed in cages next to each other. A small harmless puff of air was directed at the mother. The hens didn't respond because they knew it was harmless. When the researchers aimed the puff of air at the chicks, the hens became upset. It would seem the hen knew the puff of air would be unpleasant to her chicks and she became upset for them.

By just watching your own flock you will see a wide range of emotions. The joy of finding an extra special treat. Jealousy of a flock mate getting more attention from you or a rooster. Sadness at being picked on by others. It is important to keep in mind, chickens are NOT bird brains. They feel, remember, and make choices based on their past experiences. Never underestimate a chicken's ability to understand.

How to Train Your Chickens

Chicken keepers who have birds that come running to them, jump in their laps, and that enjoy a good cuddle, know it is the result of time and patience. The chickens know they can trust their keeper because they have been shown love, care, and respect from day one. The most important part of training your flock is trust. It is a simple thing but it takes time, effort, and patience to build. It is easier to build trust with day-old chicks than a full-grown chicken who has already formed opinions about the world around them. That doesn't mean you can't train older birds, it just means it is going to take longer and will require some commitment from you to be patient and go at the chicken's pace.

Much of a chicken's behavior is inherent, meaning they are born just knowing it, but they do need to learn some skills in order to survive. Chickens will copy each other and this is an important part of the learning process. When a bird sees another pecking at something, it will copy, thus learning what to eat, and where to find food and water. It also means that other chickens can learn new skills you teach them from each other! This makes the training process a bit easier.

To start taming your chickens you should begin by being quiet and moving slowly around them. All chicks will be skittish at first. It is an inherent behavior to run and stay safe. Sudden movements or loud noises can startle the chicks, causing a fight-or-flight response. If you move slowly and pick them up gently, they will learn not to be afraid of you.

You will want to spend time holding and interacting with your new chicks. You will want to sit when doing this so that your chicks will be safe. This way if you accidentally drop a chick or it jumps from your hand, it doesn't fall very far. Chickens have hollow bones that make chicks very fragile. As you both begin to relax, you can place the chick in your lap, keeping one hand near at all times.

Gently stroke your chick's head, neck, and back. This will get them used to being touched. Some chicks really enjoy being petted and may even make a trill sound like a cat purr. As your chicks become more comfortable around you, they may even fall asleep on you. This is a good sign that they are learning that human contact is not only okay, but something to look forward to.

Everyone has their favorites, but if you want your whole flock to be tame, then you need to handle all of the chicks equally. We usually hold our chicks in the evening as a family activity with each person taking one to hold and sit with. Within just a few weeks you will begin to notice that your chicks not only put up with being handled, they begin to look forward to spending time with you. They will start looking for you when they hear your voice, they will stop and look at you when you come to the brooder, instead of trying to get away from your hand.

At about a month old you can begin giving your flock small treats. Treats are perfect to use as positive reinforcement. What does that mean? Using positive reinforcement to train your chickens means you reward the behaviors you like and ignore the behaviors you do not like. If you keep training sessions short and upbeat, positive reinforcement training can be fun for you and your chickens. Once chickens know that training leads to lots of good things for them, many begin to view training sessions as playtime.

When teaching your chicken new behaviors or tricks, you will need to give them a cue or signal to let them know what to do. Chickens are very visual, so placing an item in front of them will draw their attention. For example, if you want a chicken to peck a xylophone, you would need to start with target training. Chickens are attracted to red, so the chicken would likely peck the red key first. Every time the chicken pecks at a key, you can give them a small treat, like a mealworm.

To get the chicken to associate the reward with the correct behavior, the treat or praise must be given immediately. In many zoo settings, trainers use "bridges" to signal that the animal did the right thing. The signal bridges the gap in time between the moment the bird performed the behavior and the actual moment they get the reward. Trainers will often blow a whistle or use a clicker to bridge the time it takes to hand over the treat. For chickens, I suggest a clicker, which isn't as startling to birds as a whistle.

You can also train a chicken to go through a hoop. This is called capture training, meaning you reward the chicken when it does a normal behavior you want them to repeat. You are capturing that behavior and making it an enjoyable one to do on command. For hoop training you will want to set up the hoop on the ground so the chicken can easily walk through it. Next you wait. You may have to wait a while for the chicken to walk through the hoop but as soon as it does, you give the bridge signal and the treat. You can try enticing the chicken through the hoop with treats, but always give the bridge signal before the treat so they realize they did something good.

When training, never chase, hit, or yell at your chickens, as you will lose any trust you had with them. Training can be frustrating, and patience is important. Also, be aware that chickens are able to understand that when an object is taken away and hidden from them, it still exists. Most human toddlers don't get this concept. So, when you hide the treats you use for training, your chickens are smart enough to know they still exist and will peck your pockets or whatever container you put them in.

For older chickens who have never really interacted with humans one-on-one, it will take weeks to months to build their trust. You will have to start by getting them comfortable with you being around. This may mean sitting in your run quietly reading a book, not even paying attention to them. Once chickens become used to you, you can start tossing them small treats. This teaches them that good things come from this strange human. Over time you can get the chickens to come close enough to eat out of your hand. When they peck your hand, it might surprise you but it shouldn't hurt, so try to stay still. Once the chickens are comfortable eating out of your hand, you can slowly reach out and gently touch them. Do not grab them and pick them up. This will scare them and all the trust you have built will be gone. With time and patience, sooner or later one or two will begin jumping into your lap. The key with older chickens is take your time, go slow, and let the chickens show you how they feel about the whole situation.

Showing Your Birds in Competition

There are many organizations out there that can teach you about your chickens and allow you to show them in competition.

Think dog show for birds! Both of my sons are in 4H and the oldest is also in FFA (Future Farmers of America). Both programs are a great way to get started in competing— whether showing off your chickens or your knowledge of chickens.

There are also national organizations such as the American Poultry Association that hold shows.

Going to your first poultry show can be a bit overwhelming. There are so many chickens of different breeds you won't know where to look first! Don't worry, they are usually well-organized and people will be happy to point you in the right direction. Poultry shows aren't just a place to show off your chickens, they are great places to find specific breeds to add to your flock, to make new friends, and gain new knowledge.

If you plan to show your chickens, you will need to understand how a show works. Chickens are judged on a point system determined by the APA. The closer the chicken is to the standard of perfection, the better it will do in the show. Be aware that chickens can be disqualified from showing if they don't meet their breed standard. Also keep in mind, not all breeds are recognized by the APA in competition.

Chickens are separated into categories to compete by size, then by breed. Next, they are broken down by color. Yes, some breeds come in different colors! Last, they are broken down by gender and age. In each class the judge goes over each and every chicken, comparing it to the standard of perfection. The judge will pick the best in each class who will then compete for the best in their breed. At the end of shows the judges will pick the best of the best and award Best in Show.

Poultry shows aren't just about judging chickens. Oftentimes there will be showmanship competitions. This is a chance for young keepers to show the judges just how much they know about chickens and demonstrate how to properly handle their birds. Contestants all line up at the judging table where the judge asks general poultry questions. The judge will ask about your bird and how you care for it. They may ask you to handle your chicken and point out the different body parts. At the end the judge will hand out ribbons.

The nice thing about showmanship is you don't need a show-quality chicken. You just need a chicken that is calm and will stand still for you! You will need to dress nice. Most poultry judges like black pants with a white button shirt. Some contestants will wear white show coats that look like lab coats. Many people ask how to do well in showmanship and while knowing your facts is important, many judges look for kids who are enjoying themselves. Always make eye contact with the judge when you are answering questions, and be sure to smile.

How to Give a Chicken a Bath

Sometimes your chicken might get super dirty and need a bath, but usually bathing a chicken is done for competition. Remember, you want your chicken to look the best it can, all clean and fluffed, to make a good impression with the judges. Bathing a chicken is pretty easy to do, just remember the chicken might be a little nervous the first time.

To wash your chicken you will need water, Dawn dish soap, some towels, and a blow dryer. Begin by wetting the chicken's feathers with soapy water. Make sure to get dirty areas nice and wet so that you can gently use your fingers to remove dirt and poop from the chicken's feathers. Next you will want to completely rinse your chicken to get all the soap off. Gently

squeeze water off the chicken like you would do with your own hair in the shower. When you take the chicken out of the water, wrap it in a towel to absorb more water from the feathers.

Now comes the "fun" part of blowing dry your chicken. Some chickens don't like the blow dryer, while others will relax completely. If your chicken doesn't like the blow dryer, try to keep the wings wrapped in a towel for as long as possible while you work on other areas of the body. This will cut down on a lot of flapping. You will want the dryer set on WARM, not hot. Also, make sure the dryer is on the lowest setting so the air is gentle and doesn't startle the chicken. Keep the dryer moving at all times so your chicken doesn't become uncomfortable due to the heat. It should take about five minutes to fully dry your chicken this way.

If you are bathing your chicken for competition, the bath should happen just before show day. Once clean, keep the washed show birds on clean bedding till competition so that they have less of a chance of soiling their good looks. You can keep baby wipes handy at competitions in case your chicken makes a little mess on their feathers that needs to be cleaned off fast.

12

More Flock Fun!

Easy Egg Recipes

One of the exciting things about raising chickens are all the amazing eggs you get. But what do you do with all of those eggs? Here are some super easy recipes you can try with some of those eggs your chickens are giving you.

Hard-Boiled Eggs

Being able to make hard-boiled eggs opens a world of culinary opportunities. Hard-boiled eggs are super easy to make. Start with room temperature eggs. If you have refrigerated your eggs, let them sit on the counter for 20 minutes before you begin.

Never overfill your pot with eggs. The water needs to be able to circulate around them.

Start by filling a pot full of water and place it on high heat on the stovetop till it begins to boil. Once the water begins to boil, use a large spoon to gently lower the eggs into the water. Turn the heat down to a simmer and set a timer for 12 minutes. Don't worry if you let the water boil a little too much or leave your eggs in a little long, it's okay.

Once the eggs have boiled, drain the water and place the eggs in the refrigerator to cool. If you are in a hurry you can cool the eggs in ice water. When you are ready to eat or use, tap the fat end of the egg on the counter to crack the shell and peel. If you are having a hard time getting the shell off, put the egg under cold running water as you peel.

So, what can you do with a boiled egg other than eat it? Hard boiled eggs can be chopped up and used on salads. They can also be deviled, or turned into a sandwich spread!

Deviled Eggs

12 large eggs, hard-boiled and
  cooled
½ cup mayonnaise
2 tablespoons mustard
Salt and black pepper to taste

Slice the hard-boiled eggs in half lengthwise. Next, scoop

the yolks into a bowl and combine the remaining ingredients to make your filling. Fill the egg-white halves with the yolk mixture using a spoon or resealable plastic bag with a corner snipped.

Some people like to add a little relish to the mix and sprinkle paprika on top as a garnish. Keep deviled eggs in an airtight container in the refrigerator till you serve them.

Egg Salad

One of our favorite things to make after Easter is a bunch of egg salad sandwiches. But you don't have to wait for Easter to boil up a bunch of eggs and make these yummy sandwiches. It's great on crackers as well.

8 eggs, hard-boiled and cooled
½ cup mayonnaise
1 teaspoon yellow mustard
¼ teaspoon paprika
Salt and pepper to taste

Start by chopping up the hard-boiled eggs, just like you would to use them as a salad topping. Place the chopped eggs in a bowl, and stir in the mayonnaise and mustard. Season with salt, pepper, and paprika. Stir and serve on your favorite sandwich bread or crackers.

Scrambled Eggs

Scrambled eggs on the stove are an easy and popular breakfast dish. You can eat them plain or add in your favorite items. I love to top my scrambled eggs with some Colby Jack cheese!

4 eggs
¼ cup milk
Salt and pepper to taste
2 tsp. butter

Start by cracking 4 eggs into a bowl and add in the milk, salt, and pepper. Stir the ingredients well, so that everything is well blended. Place a large nonstick skillet over medium heat and melt butter. Pour the egg mixture into the pan.

As the eggs begin to cook, gently pull the eggs across the pan with a spatula, forming large soft piles. Keep pulling, lifting, and folding eggs until no visible liquid remains. Remove from heat and serve.

French Toast

Eggs can turn a simple slice of bread into an extraordinary breakfast.

2 eggs
⅔ cup milk
¼ teaspoon ground cinnamon
1 teaspoon vanilla extract
6 thick slices of bread

Start by cracking two eggs in a bowl. Beat the eggs together with the milk, cinnamon, and vanilla. Heat a lightly oiled griddle or skillet over medium-high heat. Dunk each slice of bread in the egg mixture, soaking both sides. Place the bread in a pan, and cook on both sides until golden. Serve hot.

Egg Breakfast Bites

These breakfast bites are not only easy to make, but are also fun to eat!

28–32 oz. bag tator tots
8 eggs
½ cup milk
Cheddar cheese
Choice of toppings like ham,
    bacon, and vegetables

Start by preheating the oven to 400°F. Grab your muffin pans and spray them with cooking spray. Pop your frozen tator tots in the microwave for a couple minutes to thaw them.

Place 3–4 tator tots in the bottom of each muffin hole, smashing them down to make the bottom of the breakfast bites. Put the muffin pan in the oven for 10 minutes while you get the rest of the ingredients ready. Chop up any vegetables or cook any meat your plan to put in. Mix your eggs and milk and whisk completely.

After 10 minutes, remove the pans and turn the oven temperature down to 350°F. Add your chopped toppings to each muffin hole and pour equal amounts of your egg mix over the top. Finish with a sprinkle of cheese. Bake for 20 minutes and enjoy! If your bites stick to the pan, use a butter knife to go around the edges to loosen them up. Leftover bites can be stored in an airtight container in the refrigerator and rewarmed in the microwave.

Boredom Busters for Your Flock

If you keep your chickens in a run, or if they stay inside a lot during the winter because of bad weather, you will need to help keep your flock entertained. A bored flock can cause all sorts of trouble like feather pecking each other, or breaking and eating their own eggs. It is really easy to make boredom buster treats and activities from things you can find around your own home!

Piñata Party and Garlands

Fun and healthy treats can help your flock beat boredom. Hanging food for your flock can give them hours of entertainment. There are companies that sell food holders, but with some sturdy twine or wire, you can put together all sorts of fun boredom busters for your flock.

To make your flock a piñata, simply grab a head of cabbage and wrap it in twine to hang it. For an apple, core it to remove the seeds which contain cyanide, and run a string through the hole. For other fruits and vegetables, you can poke a hole through them with a skewer or use a drill to make a hole to string them up for hanging.

To create a festive garland, you can put twine or wire through the food. Brussels sprouts, cranberries, grapes, zucchini, beets, and banana and apple slices not only look great together, your flock will think they taste great too! Use your imagination and have fun making your flock all sorts of combinations of piñatas and garlands to keep them busy and add a festive mood to your coop!

Treat Balls

The key to a good boredom buster is being interactive and requiring the chickens to work to get the rewards. While you could buy a treat ball online or at the feed store, you can easily make your own with a used water bottle!

Use a drill to put holes in a used water bottle and fill with treats such as mealworms and seeds. Chickens will have to peck and kick at the bottle to get it to move so the treats will fall out the holes. Once the bottle is discovered by your flock, sit back and watch as different members of your flock test their skills. You will soon discover some members are smarter than others and some may even team up to keep the bottle moving so even more treats drop out.

Play "Frisbee"

While salt crackers are not the best treats, we discovered our chickens were amazing at "frisbee" when the kids were eating some outside. When they threw a cracker like a frisbee, the entire flock would take off running, anticipating where it might land. Believe it or not, they were really good at guessing where the "frisbee" would land! Tossing treats to your flock is a great way to burn off energy, provide exercise, and just have a good time.

Grapes are a healthy "frisbee" you can toss for your flock. Running after and stealing grapes from each other is not only an enjoyable pastime for your flock, but you might end up giggling a bit too. My husband once flung a pancake out back and you have never seen something as funny as a flock of chickens and ducks streaking across the yard after it!

DIY Dust Bath Spa

Chickens love to take dust baths. While a free range flock can find their own areas to do their spa activities, you may not want them to dig holes in your yard. If you keep your flock in a run, providing a dust bath area is important not only for normal feather cleaning, but also for preventing pests like mites.

Keep in mind, dust bathing usually turns into a group activity, so make sure your DIY dust bath spa is big enough for more than one chicken. Once one chicken starts flopping in the dirt, everyone else seems unable to resist joining in! You can use items you find around your home to create the "spa." An old apple crate, large tire, kiddy pool, or outgrown sandbox would make the perfect container for a dust bath area.

Once you have the container in place, it's time to add in the dust bath elements. For the most part, it will be made up of plain old dry dirt. If you buy soil to fill your container, make sure it doesn't contain fertilizers or chemicals. You can add in a little sand to help keep the soil loose. You can also add in wood ash from your fireplace or food grade diatomaceous earth. Either of these will help with preventing and treating mites.

Once the dust bath spa is completed, it's time to grab a chair and sit back and enjoy the show. Watching your flock throw dirt on each other, flopping and rolling around, and shaking off clouds of dust is great entertainment! You and your flock will have hours of enjoyment.

Chicken Jungle Gym

Exercise is an important activity for humans and chickens. If you keep your flock in a run, you will need to provide them with ways to get enough exercise. A great way to do this is to build them a jungle gym! Chickens are able to jump up 2 feet, higher if they can get lift with their wings. That means you can make a multilevel play area for them.

The best way to start is from the ground up and think like a chicken. Place small rocks for them to hop over and walk around. Place small logs and stumps for them to hop up on. You can place branches, roost bars, and platforms higher up for them to explore. Just keep in mind your chickens will need to be able to leap from level to level so keep the tiers going up closer together or install walkways from platform to platform. Chickens have hollow bones and injury can occur if they fall too far, so keep your jungle gym under 5 feet tall.

Flock Blocks

A flock block is a large, solid block of chicken treats. While there are commercially ready-made flock blocks you can buy, it's way more fun to make your own. The fun part is that you get to pick what to put in your block, like a mad scientist!

A basic flock block recipe has around 5 cups of "dry" ingredients and 1 cup of "wet" ingredients. While the wet ingredients stay the same, the dry ingredients can be made up of lots of different things, including grains, fruits, and seeds.

So, what does a recipe look like?

Dry Ingredients

2 cups scratch grains
1 cup old fashioned oats
1 cup cornmeal
¼ cup wheat germ
½ cup raisins or cranberries
½ cup sunflower seeds

Wet Ingredients

½ cup molasses
½ cup coconut oil, tallow, or lard
3 eggs plus their crushed shells

Preheat the oven to 350°F. In a large bowl mix your dry ingredients together before adding in the wet ingredients. Make sure it is mixed well. Pour your mixture into two greased 8-inch cake pans. Using your finger, make a hole near one edge so you will have a way to string it up if you want. Bake for around 30 minutes. You want the center to be firm to the touch. Use a butter knife around the inside rim of each pan and turn over to remove the block. Let it cool completely before serving. Extra blocks can be refrigerated or wrapped and frozen for later use.

Chicken Pops

Chickens don't handle extreme heat very well, but you can help them by whipping up a batch of chicken popsicles! These summertime treats provide nice cold water in the form of ice along with taste treats your flock will love to get their beaks on.

Start by chopping up the fruits or veggies you want to include in your pops. The higher the water content in the food, the better. Remember, we are trying to help the chickens stay cool! Some favorites to include are peas, cucumber, green beans, strawberries (including the tops), blueberries, cranberries, raisins, and watermelon.

Now you could make one big frozen treat for the flock to share by using a larger pan like a bread pan, but it is really fun to use an ice cube tray to make individual pops so they don't have to compete with each other for the food. Fill the pan or ice cube tray holes with your chopped-up food and add water to top them off. Remember water expands when it freezes so don't overfill your ice cube tray holes!

When your pops are frozen, you can serve them right away or you can make a bunch and put the extras in a freezer bag to keep on hand for the next hot day!

Gardening with and for Chickens

Chickens love to garden as much as humans do. They love to till the soil with their feet, clear bugs with their beaks, and eat all the yummy produce. And while it may be fun to hang out with your flock in your garden, chickens have no manners! They will dig up your seeds, inhale your baby plants, dust bathe in your raised beds, poop everywhere, and leave your garden looking like a tornado hit!

When gardening with chickens, timing and supervision is a must if you want any of the produce from your garden to make it to your dining table. Since our flock free ranges, we have a fence around our garden. We also have rules as to when our chickens are allowed in the garden area.

Spring is the perfect time for your flock to join you in the garden. As you turn the soil, they will follow you around looking for worms and bugs. Chicken feet do a great job of fluffing the soil as they scratch. We usually let our flock hang out in the garden, digging, bug hunting, and nibbling weeds until it is time to plant. Once the seeds and starter plants go into the garden, the gate to our garden closes till fall, so that our flock doesn't destroy all our hard work. In the fall, after we harvest the last bits of food, we leave the gate open till spring. Our flock spends many happy fall days eating bugs, the plants, and any last produce we missed.

Composting Your Coop

While our flock may not be IN the garden during the summer months, they still help us garden. Composting is a simple way to turn waste, like chicken poop and litter, into wonderful fertilizer for your garden. Chicken poop is high in ammonia, so it will need to be composted before putting it on your garden or it could kill your plants.

A compost pile can be as simple as a pile, or you can create or buy a bin to keep it in. We used old wood pallets to create a contained area. A compost pile needs "Green" material like kitchen scraps, coffee grounds, fresh grass clippings, and chicken poop. You also need "Brown" material like dead leaves, straw, sawdust, shredded newspaper, and paper towels.

It is important that your compost pile stays moist but not soggy. It should be placed where it can get a lot of sunlight to help all the materials break down. Odor in a compost pile comes from overly moist and matted green material. If you notice an odor, you can add in more "brown" and "turn" your pile. You will need to "turn" the pile every now and then with a pitchfork anyway. This introduces oxygen deeper into the pile, helps it dry out, and speeds up the decomposition process.

Sharing is Caring!

During the summer months, whenever we weed the garden, we make sure to throw all the weeds over the garden fence to our flock. Since they share their poop for our compost, we share what grows with them and chickens LOVE weeds.

You could also set up a mini garden just for your flock! You can locate this next to your run or somewhere you don't mind them getting into. In addition to most herbs you can grow, chickens love leafy greens. If you grow a chicken garden next to your run, include plants that will climb your run, like peas, as they will provide shade while also providing food. Gardening doesn't always have to be a ground-level activity, think up!

Plants Chickens Love

Herbs: basil, bee balm, lavender, lemon balm, mint, oregano, parsley, rosemary, sage

Flowers: bee balm, calendula, nasturtium, sunflowers, viola

Vegetables: beets, broccoli, cabbage, cucumbers, kale, lettuce, peas, pumpkins, spinach, watermelon

Fruit: blueberries, raspberries, strawberries

Sprouts

Winter for us means lots of snow and bitter cold. It makes it impossible to grow things in our garden. Our chickens miss the fresh produce as much as we do, that's why we grow sprouts for them indoors. Growing sprouts is fun, easy, and a great way to provide your flock with greens during the long months of winter. While you can buy sprouts at the grocery store, it is much less expensive to grow your own.

You will need:

- 2 containers, one with holes in it for drainage. You can make your own by buying plastic containers at the dollar store and using a nail and hammer to punch holes in the bottom. Make sure the holes are smaller than your seeds.
- Seeds to sprout; examples include . . .
  Seeds: sesame, sunflower, buckwheat, or pumpkin
  Legumes: mung beans, lentils, chickpeas, or green peas
  Grains: barley, corn, wheat, quinoa, oats, or rye
  Vegetable seeds: alfalfa, clover, radish, kale, cabbage, or turnip
- Water

Begin by placing your seeds in a large bowl and soaking them in water overnight. You will want to soak your seeds 8–24 hours before draining them and moving them to your sprouting container. Layer your seeds so they are no more than ½-inch thick. You will want to put a second container under the first to catch any dripping.

For the next five to seven days you will want to rinse and drain your seed sprouts every morning and evening. Drain them thoroughly to encourage germination and growth. Your container should be kept between 50–70°F and be located in a spot that gets good sunlight. When the sprouts are three to four inches long, they are ready to be fed to your flock. And trust me, in the dead of winter, they will gobble them gone in no time!

Chicken Crafts

Not only does our family love chickens, we love making crafts too! It is fun to make chicken related crafts, but it is also fun to make crafts with and for your flock. So, grab your crafting supplies and try out a few of our favorite craft ideas. They are chicken tested and mother approved!

Rocking Chicken Flock

Supplies
Paper plates
1 sheet red craft paper
1 sheet yellow craft paper
Googly eyes
Scissors
Glue

To make a rocking chicken, you will need two paper plates. Fold one plate in half to make the body. Make sure the beveled edge curves out from the fold. Cut the second plate into quarters. This will be enough pieces to make four tails. Take one of the four pieces and fold it in half and glue it to form the tail. You can cut the tail edge in curves or strips to make it look more like a tail.

Next you will need to cut out a comb and a wattle from the red craft paper and a beak from the yellow craft paper. Grab your glue and glue the tail and comb to the back side of the chicken. Next glue the beak and wattle to the inside crease of the paper plate (see picture). Last, add a googly eye to complete the chicken. When you place your chicken upright and tap the tail, it will rock back and forth like it's walking or pecking!

Origami Chick Bookmark

Supplies

Yellow craft paper
Orange craft paper
Scissors
Glue
Black marker

Take a sheet of yellow craft paper and cut it in half. Use one half to make your bookmark. Start by folding over one corner to create a triangle. Cut off the excess and turn your triangle so the long edge is at the bottom and the right angle faces up.

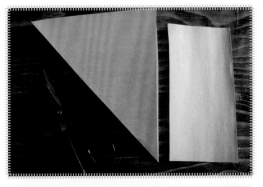

Next, fold the lower right corner up to meet the top right-angled corner. Then take the left lower corner and fold it up to meet the top right-angled corner.

Fold these two back open. Flip down one of the top sheets and crease.

Now fold the flaps you created back up and tuck into your bookmark.

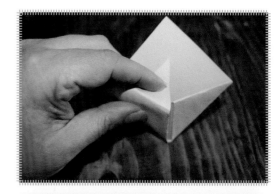

Use your scissors to slightly round the pointy corners on the book mark.

With the orange paper, cut out a beak and two feet. The feet can be made out of little heart shapes. Glue them on to your book mark and then add on the eyes with a black marker.

Now you can mark your reading book with a cute little feathered friend any time you need to take a break!

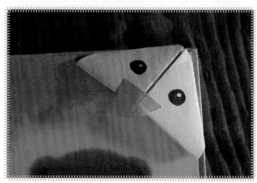

Chicken Pot

Why not make some herb pots that look like chickens to plant yummy treats in for your chickens?! Bring a little whimsy to your coop and run area. You can buy terra-cotta pots at any home improvement or hardware store and with a little acrylic paint and your imagination, you can make these adorable pots perfect for growing herbs for your flock.

Supplies

Terra-cotta pots of
   different sizes
Acrylic paint
Paint brushes
Clear sealing spray

When painting your pots, keep in mind that terra-cotta loves to soak up paint, so make sure you get a good cover on your body coat of paint. You can make your chickens white for larger "adult" sized pots and yellow for "chick" sized pots. After you paint on faces, spray the outside of the pots with a clear sealing spray to keep your artwork safe from the rain. Now just fill the pots with soil and plant your favorite herbs! Simple, fun, and rewarding for both you and your flock!

Blown Egg Ornament

When my son's first hen laid her first egg, he was super excited. She laid pretty blueish green eggs and I knew exactly what to do with it. I wanted him to be able to keep it forever, so I blew it out and made a Christmas ornament out of it. Years later, he still has his egg!

Blowing out an egg isn't as hard as people thing. You can buy special kits to do it, but you really just need a push pin and a paperclip. Seriously! That and a lot of air in your lungs.

Supplies
Egg
Push pin
Paper clip
Bowl
Button
Ribbon
Glue

Start by gently but firmly pushing the push pin into one end of the egg. Turn the pin back and forth between your fingers as you push, like a drill. Once the pin is in the egg, rotate it around the hole to open it up a little. Now repeat this on the other end of the egg so you have two holes.

Once you have your holes, take the unbent paper clip, stick it in the egg, and start moving it around. Scramble the egg up for a minute and you should see egg membrane start to ooze out the bottom hole. Now make a seal with your mouth on the egg and blow. If you scrambled your egg well, it should all slide out quick and easy.

Once your egg is empty, you need to rinse it. Carefully run water over it and a little will go in the holes. Shake the water in the egg, empty it, and let your egg dry. Once dry, you can decorate and add a hanger to your egg. I attached a ribbon to a button and then glued the button on one end of the egg.

Feather Ornament

Chickens have such beautiful feathers and it always seems so sad at molting time to watch all those feathers blow away. We collect up some of those feathers for crafting with and making ornaments. Craft stores carry clear ornament balls that you can fill with your favorite things, and for us, that means feathers!

You will need to collect the smaller feathers so that they will fit in your ornament ball. Smaller feathers are also more flexible so they are easier to move around inside the ornament. We use wooden skewers to help move the feathers around inside the ball. You can mix and match the feathers or, as we

do, make an ornament for each of our flock members with their feathers. We also add in plastic snow to give the feathers a more Christmassy feeling. These also make unique gifts to give at Christmas time too!

Chicken Painting

Call me crazy, but one day it hit me . . . why paint a picture of a chicken, when you can have a chicken paint a picture for you? How many people can say they have artwork done by their chicken?! This activity is one that will take a little patience and should be done outside.

Supplies
Paper
Acrylic paint
Paper plates
Treats
Soap and water to clean up

I've found the best way to set up this activity is to get a plastic shower curtain at the dollar store and spread it out on the ground before you start. Next you will want to place pieces of paper on the plastic. You can use small pebbles to hold them down if there is a breeze. Next you will want to put acrylic paint on the paper plates so that the chickens can step on them and coat their feet. Place the paper plates around the blank papers.

Now for the fun part, getting your chickens to walk through the paint and onto the paper. You can place your chickens' feet on the paint-covered paper plates, or you can hope they step on them on their own. Treats are what will motivate your flock to walk around with painted feet. Sprinkle mealworms or other treats around the papers so your chickens will walk across the paper to get to them.

It will seem like total chaos as they strut around, pecking treats and walking with painted feet across the paper. Make sure to use soapy water and clean your chickens' feet off when they are done. When it is all over, you will end up with one-of-a-kind artwork to frame and hang on your wall!

The end

INDEX

4H, 35, 205

A

abdomen, health, 149
age, 42, 138, 140–141
aging, 73
    agility, 74
    challenges of older hens,
        73–74
    and flock, 73
    mobility, 74
    modification, 75
Ameraucana
    climate, 18
    comb, 16
    egg color, 32–33
American Poultry
    Association (APA), 27, 205.
    See also Sexing
amino acids, 22, 53
ammonia, 61, 82, 224
Amprolium, 60, 110, 157
anatomy, 9–26
anemia, 168–169
antibiotics, 143, 159
Appenzeller Spitzhauben
    climate, 20
appetite, 153, 157, 165
arthritis, 74
Australorp, 34
    climate, 18

color, 34
comb, 15
egg color, 34
eggs, 29, 34
feathers, 34
meat, 29
parenting, 34
personality, 34
size, 34
avian flu, 152–153, 173

B

bacteria, 89, 132, 143, 150,
    153–154
bacterial yeast infection, 174
balance, 176
bantam birds, 28, 31
    advantages of, 31
    cold temperatures, 29–30
    coop, 31
    eggs, 31
    pros and cons, 31
    sexing, 31
    weight, 31
Barred Rock
    climate, 20
    eggs, 29
    laying, 71
    meat, 29
baths, 207–208
beak, 63

crossed beak, 63
    health, 148
    rubbing, 189
bedding, 53, 61, 89, 92–93,
    162, 168, 186, 193, 208
    chicks, 51
bedtime, 13
begging, 98
biosecurity, 149–150, 166–167
Black Sumatra
    climate, 20
bleach, 61, 90
bleeding, 70, 156, 161
blood, 124
blow drying, 208
Blown Egg Ornament,
    232–233
bobcats, 100, 106–107
body
    mass, 18, 20
    temperature, 11, 14, 22, 30,
        129, 163–166
boredom, 5, 28, 77, 82, 97, 160,
    217–222
botulism, 153–154
Brahma, 35
    climate, 18, 20, 35
    color, 35
    egg color, 33
    eggs, 29, 35
    handling, 35

meat, 35
parenting, 35
size, 35
breathing issues. *See*
Respiratory or breathing
issues
breeds, 5
choice of, 27–40
and climate, 17–18, 20
cold hardy, 18
dual-purpose, 29, 40
egg layers, 29
heat tolerant, 20
hybrid, 58
for kids, 34–40
meat production, 29
mixing, 42
number of, 27
ornamental, 39
sex-linked, 58
Brewer's yeast, 61
brooder, 49–50, 65–67
bedding, 51
cleaning, 55–56, 61
safety, 54–55
temperature, 54
broody, 36, 124, 137,
191–193, 195
breaking, 193
and pecking, 192
Buckeye
climate, 18
Buff Orpington, 32, 34–36
climate, 18, 35
color, 35
egg color, 33, 35
eggs, 35
personality, 32, 34–36
bugs, 12, 77, 95, 97, 223
bullying, 5, 97
bumblefoot, 154–155
butchering, 26

C
caffeine, 116

calcium, 112, 116, 126, 139–140,
158–159, 174
candling, 47–49
cannibalism, 120
cardiac issues, 115–116
catching chickens, 69
cats, 100, 106–107
ceca, 122–123
cecal worms, 175
cedar shavings, 51, 61
Chantecler
comb, 16
chick, 9
bedding, 51
behavior, 66
cleaning, 55–56
dust bath, 187
enrichment, 55
feed, 110
flying, 67
food, 51, 53
handling, 56–57
perching, 67
selecting, 42
sexing, 57–59
sleeping, 65–66
starter, 53
tail feathers, 67
talking to, 57
training, 201–202
warmth, 53–54
water, 51–53
wing feathers, 66
chick, hatching, 44–49
brooder, 49
candling, 47–49
eggs, fertilized, 44
embryo, 47
incubator, 44–46
lockdown, 48
pecking order, 182
time, 47, 49
Chicken Painting, 235–236
chicken pops, 222
Chicken Pot, 231

chicken wire, 96
choking, 55
cleaning up, 2, 6. *See also*
Brooder, cleaning up;
Coop, cleaning; Nest box,
cleaning
eggs, 132–133
cleanliness, 6
climate, 17–18, 20, 29–30, 35,
40, 162–163
cloaca, 122–123
coccidia, 60
coccidiosis, 53, 60, 110, 123,
156–157
Cochin, 36
climate, 18
color, 36
comb, 15
egg color, 33, 36
eggs, 36
parenting, 36
personality, 36
sizes, 36
cock. *See* Roosters
cockatrice, 142
cockerel, 10
color, 20
comb, 10–11, 14–18, 20, 40,
58, 67
aging, 74
buttercup, 15–16
cushion, 15–16
frostbite, 29
health, 147, 153, 156, 161–162,
168, 176
and laying, 72
and leadership, 17
and location, 16
and mates, 16–17
pea, 15–16
rose, 15, 40
sexing, 58
single, 15
strawberry, 15
and temperature, 18, 29–30

temperature regulation, 30
v-shaped, 15–16
walnut, 15–16
communication, 181
community, 3–4
compost, 6, 93, 224
coop, 3–6, 77–93
chores, daily, 92
chores, weekly, 93
chores, yearly, 93
cleaning, 82, 90–93
converting existing
structure, 81
designs, 79
doors, 82, 92
drafts, 81, 162
drainage, 78
dropping board, 85, 93
entering, 67–68
grow-out pen, 80
heating, 91
isolation coop, 80
kits, 79
laws, 78
light, 82, 136–137, 160
litter, 85
location, 78
locking at night, 92
mobile, 79–80, 93
nest box, 86–87
permanent, 79, 82
pre-built, 81
and predators, 79–80, 82
roost area, 84–85
semimobile, 81
shade, 78
size, 4–5, 28, 31, 79
sturdiness, 79
styles, 79–81
sunlight, 78
ventilation, 82
window, 82
Cornish
comb, 16
Cornish Cross

meat, 29
cost, 2
counter-peristalsis
contraction, 141
coyote, 100, 106–107
crafts, 227–236
Blown Egg Ornament,
232–233
Chicken Painting, 235–236
Chicken Pot, 231
Feather Ornament, 234–235
Origami Chick Bookmark,
228–230
Rocking Chicken Flock,
227–228
cramps, 115
crop, 10–11, 116, 122–123
sour and impacted, 173–174
crossed beak, 63
crowing, 58–59
curled toes, 62–63
cyanide, 116

D
dead animals, 154
death, 74–75
deciding if chickens are right
for you, 2
Delaware
climate, 18, 20
Department of Natural
Resources, 104–105
Deviled Eggs, 212–213
diarrhea, 60, 115–116, 146, 149,
153, 156, 176
diatomaceous earth (DE),
90–91, 168–169, 171, 188
digestion, 122–124
disease. *See* Illness
disinfectant, 149–150
diurnal, 13
dogs, 99–100, 106–107
dominance. *See* Pecking
order
Dominique

comb, 15
down, 23
sexing, 58
dreams, 198–199
drowning, 52
dust baths, 22, 55, 66, 95,
185–188
DIY spa, 218–220
purpose, 187

E
E. coli, 143
ears, 11
Easter Egger, 36–37
climate, 18, 20
egg color, 36
personality, 36–37
size, 36
eating, 1
egg-bound, 157–160
Egg Breakfast Bites, 215–216
egg production, 73, 126, 172,
176
and age, 138
and broodiness, 137
and illness, 138
and molting, 136, 197
and predators, 138
and stress, 137
and weather, 137
and winter, 136–137, 160
eggs, 1–2, 28–29, 34–40, 125–
143. *See also* Laying
and aging, 158
air sac, 129–130
albumen, 128–130
amount, 71
bantam birds, 31, 125
bloom, 129, 132
blue, 32–33, 36
brown, 32–33, 37
brown, chocolate, 32–33
brown, light, 33
chalazae, 128, 130
checking for, 92

chick production, 72
cleaner, 132
cleaning, 132–133
cock eggs, 141
collecting, 86, 130–132
color, 32–34, 128
cycle, 127–129
egg in an egg, 141
fairy eggs, 141–142
fertilizing, 6, 44, 127
finding, 135
first, 125–127
freezing, 133–134
freshness, 132–133
freshness test, 134–135
green, 32–33, 36
and hen age, 5
lash eggs, 142–143
laying, 82
membranes, 129–130
misshaped, 139
odors, absorbing, 133
oocyte, 127–128
ovary, 128
oviduct, 128, 141, 157
ovulation, 128
pigment, 32, 128
pink, 36
refrigeration, 133
roosters, 141
rubber, 140
shells, 127–129
size, 126, 158
soft-shelled, 140
song, 72, 131, 180
spotted, 139
storing, 133–134
uniqueness, 126
warm, 129
white, 33, 128
yolk, 127–130
yolk, double, 140–141
yolk, missing, 142
Egg Salad, 213
eggshells, 112

egg tooth, 48–49, 65
Egyptian Fayoumi
    climate, 20
electrolytes, 61, 117, 166
emery board, 63
enrichment, 217–222
    chicks, 55
Epsom salts, 154–155
esophagus, 122, 173
Europe, 133–134
exercise, 77, 95, 97, 160, 187,
    193, 218, 220
eyes, 11–14, 63
    bright and clear, 42
    cones, 12–14
    eyelids, 12
    field of vision, 12
    health, 147–148, 176
    motion detection, 12, 14
    nictating membrane, 12
    night vision, 13
    retina, 14
    rods, 13
    ultraviolet light, 12, 14

F

fan, 165
farm stores, 41–43
feather, 22, 34, 38–40, 184–
    185, 194–197
    and appearance, 24
    barbs, 24, 184
    barbules, 24
    and body temperature, 22
    cleaning, 22
    color, 23
    contour, 23–24
    down, 23
    filoplume, 23–24
    follicles, 22
    growth requirements, 22
    hackle, 58
    health, 148, 154, 168, 170
    insulation, 23–24
    loss of, 22

movement of, 22
mutation, 24
nerve endings, 24
pecking, 120, 160–161, 217
pin feathers, 22, 197
quill, 22
repair, 25
semiplume, 23–24
sexing, 58
shaft, 22, 24
tail, 67
types, 23
wing, developing, 66
wing, primary flight
    feathers, 69–70
wing, trimming, 67–70
Feather Ornament, 234–235
feed, 53. *See also* Food
    medication, 53
    storage, 7
    stores, 3
feeders, 82
    cleaning, 90
    sanitizing, 93
feeding, 2
feelings, 199
    depression, 199
    empathy, 199
feet, 85
    aging, 74
    curled toes, 62–63
    health, 148, 154–155, 162
    sexing, 58
fermentation, 120–121
fertilizer, 1, 6, 93, 122
fires, 91
first aid kit, 150–152
    supplies, 151
flock, 10, 179
    block, 220–221
flying, 67, 69
food, 67, 82–83, 109–124, 165
    alcohol, 116
    apples, 116, 118
    avocado, 115

banana, 118
beans, 118
beans, raw dried, 115
berries, 118
broccoli, 118
Brussels sprouts, 118
cabbage, 118
calcium, 112
carrots, 118
cherries, 118
chick feed, 110
chicks, 51, 53
chocolate, 116
citrus, 116
coffee grounds, 116
corn, 118
corn, cracked, 119
crickets, 118
cucumber, 118
dairy products, 116
earthworms, 118
eggs, 118
fermentation, 120–121
filling, 92
fish, 118
flock block, 220–221
flowers, 225
fruit, 118, 225
garlic, 118
grains and seeds, 118
grapes, 118
grit, 113
grower feed, 110
grubs, 118
herbs, 225
layer feed, 111–112
lettuce, 118
mealworms, 118
meat, 117–118
medicated, 110
melon, 118
moldy, 117
nutrients, 109
oatmeal, 118–120
onions, 114

pasta, 118
peaches, 118
pears, 118
peas, 118
plums, 118
popcorn, 118
potatoes, 115, 118
proteins, 118
pumpkins and squash, 118
radishes, 118
raisins, 118
rhubarb, 115
rice, cooked, 118
rice, uncooked, 116
salt, 117
schedule, 111–112
scratch feed, 119
spinach, 118
sprouts, 226–227
storage, 83
sugar, 117
sunflower seeds, 118
tomato, 118
transitioning, 110
treat balls, 217
treats, 114, 149, 202
treats, amount, 117
treats, good, 117–119
turnip, 118
types, 109–110
vegetables, 225
veggies, 118
zucchini, 118
foraging, 188
fowl pox, 161
foxes, 101, 106–107
Freedom Ranger
    meat, 29
free range, 5, 28, 67–69, 77, 95,
    97–98, 135
    damage to yard, 97
    flower bed, 98
    grit, 113
    interaction with, 97–98
    poop, 98

and predators, 97
freezer camp, 26, 28–29
French Toast, 215
frisbee, 217–218
frostbite, 29, 85, 162–163
Future Farmers of America
    (FFA), 205

G
gall bladder, 122
gapeworm, 175–176
gardening, 223–227
    plants for chickens, 225
    sprouts, 226–227
gender, 27–28. *See also*
    Sexing
gizzard, 122–123
Golden Comet
    eggs, large amounts, 71
grit, 92, 113, 173

H
hackle feathers
    sexing, 58
hackles, 10–11
hairworm, 175
hand-feeding, 55
Hard-Boiled Eggs, 211–212
hatchery catalog, 32
hatching. *See* Chicks,
    hatching
hawks, 103–106
    Cooper's hawk, 103, 105
    migration, 104
    red-shouldered, 103, 105
    red-tailed, 103–105
health, 42
    checking, 92, 145
    cuddle check, 146–149
heat
    lamp, 53–54
    regulation, 14, 16, 29–30
    stress, 163–166
hemaglutin, 115
hemolytic anemia, 115

herpes virus, 171
hock, 10–11
hospital room, 151
Houdan
    comb, 16

I

illness, 59–63
    avian flu, 152–153, 173
    botulism, 153–154
    bumblefoot, 154–155
    coccidiosis, 60, 156–157
    curled toes, 62–63
    detecting, 146
    egg-bound, 157–160
    and egg production, 138
    feather pecking, 160–161
    fowl pox, 161
    frostbite, 162–163
    heat stress, 163–166
    hemolytic anemia, 115
    infectious bronchitis,
        166–167
    lash eggs, 142–143
    lice and mites, 167–171
    Marek's Disease, 63,
        171–172
    myocardial necrosis, 115
    Newcastle disease, 172
    pasty butt, 59
    pollorum, 172–173
    respiratory or breathing
        issues, 61–62
    scissor beak, 63
    sour and impacted crop,
        173–174
    spraddle leg, 62
    stargazing, 60–61
    transmission, 149–150
    vent prolapse, 174–175
    worms, 175–177
incubator, 44–46
    cleaning, 46
    humidity, 45–46
    lockdown, 48
    setting up, 46
    temperature, 45–46
    turning, 45–47
    types, 45
infectious bronchitis, 166–167
iron, 171
ISA Brown, 37
    egg color, 33, 37
    eggs, 37
    personality, 37
ivermectin, 170

J

Jersey Giant, 31
    climate, 18
    egg color, 33
jungle gym, 220

K

keel
    health, 148
keratin, 22, 25

L

large intestine, 123
laws, 2–3, 28
    changing, 3
    coop, 78
    housing, 28
    number of chickens, 28
    sex of chickens, 28
laying, 71–73, 87
    age, 73, 125, 135
    beginning, 72
    and molting, 126
    schedule, 131
    starting, 135
leadership, 5
leftovers, 1
Leghorn
    climate, 20
    comb, 15
    egg color, 33
    eggs, 29
legs, 62

aging, 74
    health, 148, 153–155, 169,
        172
    sexing, 58
lice, 167–170
    treatment, 170–171
lifespan, 5, 38, 71, 73–74
liver, 122
loudness, 6

M

mail order, 43–44
    extra chicks, 44
    minimum order, 44
Malay
    comb, 15
Marans
    climate, 18
    egg color, 32–33
Marek's Disease, 63, 123,
    171–172
mating, 73, 189
meat production, 5, 29, 40
memory, 179–180
methylxanthines
    theobromine, 116
Migratory Bird Treaty Act,
    104–105
mirror, 55
mites, 89, 148, 167–171
    northern fowl mites, 169
    red mites, 168
    scaly leg mites, 169
    treatment, 170–171
molting, 126, 136, 194–197
    age, 195
    and egg production, 197
    hard molt, 195–196
    length, 195
    schedule, 195
    soft molt, 195–196
    and stress, 195
mortality, 120
mosquitoes, 161
mourning, 74–75

Mycoplasma gallisepticum, 143
myocardial necrosis, 115
myths and facts, 6–7

N

names, 57
nest box, 72, 86–87, 135, 191
    ambience, 88
    checking for eggs, 92
    cleaning, 89–90
    contents, 89
    location, 88
    number, 88
    size, 89
nesting, 190–191
Newcastle disease, 172
new chickens, 150, 182–183
newspaper, 51, 62
nostrils
    health, 148
NPIP certification, 172–173
number of chickens, 3, 5, 28

O

obesity, 158
older chickens, 5
Olive Eggers
    egg color, 32–33
opossums, 102–103, 107
ordinance. *See* Laws
Origami Chick Bookmark,
    228–230
Orpington
    eggs, 29
outside, moving, 67–68
owls, 105–106
oyster shells, 92, 126, 159

P

panting, 14, 30, 54, 137, 163,
    166
paper towel, 51, 57, 59, 132, 224
paralysis, 63, 153, 171–172
parasites, 89, 148, 156

parenting, 34–36
Pasturella multocida, 143
pasty butt, 43, 59
pecking order, 42, 75, 181–184
    alpha, 181
    change in, 182–183
    hens, 182
    and humans, 183–184
    necessity of, 182
    rooster, 181–182
    underdog, 183
pee, 123
perching, 67, 75
persin, 115
personality, 1, 32, 34, 36–40
pet carrier, 146
pets, 50, 54
petting, 1
piñata party and garlands,
    217
pine wood shavings, 61
pip hole, 49
Plymouth Rock
    climate, 18
    egg color, 33
Polish, 38
    climate, 20
    comb, 16
    egg color, 33
    eggs, 38
    feathers, 38
    personality, 38
pollorum, 172–173
poop, 6, 56, 59, 73, 85, 92–93,
    122, 157
    blood in, 124
    cleaning, 93
    color of, 123–124
    and health, 123
    pasty, 172
    runny, 124
    samples, 176
    size, 124
positive reinforcement, 149, 202
poultry, 9

poultry shows, 3, 206
prebiotics, 53
predators, 7, 25, 74, 79–80, 82,
    95, 99–107, 138, 190
    bobcats, 100, 106–107
    cats, 100, 106–107
    checking for, 92
    dogs and coyotes, 99–100,
        106–107
    foxes, 101, 106–107
    hawks, 103–106
    identifying, 106–107
    keeping out of runs, 96
    opossums, 102–103, 107
    owls, 105–106
    raccoons, 101, 106–107
    rat, 106
    skunks, 102, 107
    snakes, 105–106
    tracks, 107
    weasels, 102, 106–107
preen gland, 10–11, 25, 184
    feather repair, 25
    oil, 25
preening, 6, 22, 184–186
Preparation H, 175
prey, 25
probiotics, 53, 60, 120, 174
pubic bones, 72, 158
pullet, 9, 27–28, 72
pyrethrum, 170

Q

quarantine, 150, 157, 168

R

raccoons, 101, 106–107
ramps, 75
rat, 106
reasons to have chickens,
    28–29
recipes
    Deviled Eggs, 212–213
    Egg Breakfast Bites,
        215–216

eggs, 211–216
Egg Salad, 213
French Toast, 215
Hard-Boiled Eggs, 211–212
Scrambled Eggs, 214
recognition, 179
research, 3–4, 9
respiratory alkalosis, 163, 172
respiratory or breathing
issues, 61–62, 153–154, 166,
172
responsibility, 2
Rhode Island Red, 38–39
climate, 18, 20
comb, 15
egg color, 33
eggs, 29
laying, 71
lifespan, 38
personality, 38–39
upkeep, 38
Rocking Chicken Flock,
227–228
rodents, 7
romance. See Mating
roost, 55, 67–68, 75, 84–85,
197–198
bars, 84–85
cleaning, 90
dropping board, 85
placement, 84
poop, 85
space, 85
roosters, 3, 6, 10, 25, 27–28, 31,
58, 67, 73, 181–182
aggressive, 26
comb, 17–18
crowing, 58–59
laws about, 28
spurs, 25–26
run, 67–68, 95
access, 96
cleaning, 93
and dust bathing, 97
grass, 81, 96

material, 96
roof, 96
shade, 164
size, 77, 96
wire, 96

S
saline solution, 61
Salmonella, 143
salpingitis, 142–143
scissor beak, 63
Scrambled Eggs, 214
scratching, 66, 95, 223
Sebright
comb, 15
seizures, 116
self-control, 180
Sevin dust, 170
sexing, 27, 57–59, 67
bantam birds, 31
comb, 58
down, 58
feet, 58
hackle feathers, 58
legs, 58
tail feathers, 58
wattles, 58
shade, 164–165
shank, 10–11
shoes, 62–63
showing competitively,
205–206
bathing, 208
breeds, 205
categories, 206
color, 206
handling, 206
point system, 205
Sicilian Buttercup
climate, 20
comb, 16
sight. See Eyes
Silkie, 39
climate, 20
comb, 16

egg color, 33
eggs, 39
feathers, 24, 39
personality, 39
size, 31
skin
health, 148
skunks, 102, 107
sleeping, 198–199, 1970198
chick, 65–66
REM phase, 198
unihemispheric slow-wave
sleep (USWS), 198
small intestine, 122
snakes, 105–106
solanine, 115
splint, 62
sports wrap, 62–63
spraddle leg, 62
spur, 10, 25–26
handling, 26
maintenance, 26
as weapon, 25
squat, 189–190
staphyloccus, 154–155
stargazing, 60–61
straight run, 28
stress, 137, 140, 195
Sultan
comb, 16
Sussex
climate, 18, 20

T
teeth, 123
temperature, 17–18, 20
thiosulphate, 114
tidbitting, 188
toes, 62–63
training, 1, 200–204
bridges, 203
chicks, 201–202
clicker, 203
cue or signal, 202–203
hoop, 203

older chickens, 204
reward, 203
treats, 202
treats, hiding, 204
travel, 2
treat balls, 217
tremors, 153
tumors, 63, 171

U

ultraviolet (UV) light, 12, 14
United States Department of
    Agriculture, 152
United States Posta
    Service, 44
University of Bristol, 179–180
upside down, 69
urban areas, 99, 101
urine, 123
urophygal gland. *See* Preen
    gland

V

vaccines
    coccidiosis, 53, 110
    fowl pox, 161
    infectious bronchitis, 166
    Marek's disease, 63, 172
vent, 10–11, 59, 122, 159
    health, 149

prolapse, 141, 174–175
Vetericyn, 155
veterinarian, 62, 143, 146, 154,
    158, 177
vinegar, white, 61, 90, 132
vitamins, 61–62, 120
vocalization, 180–181

W

water, 2, 67, 82–83, 113, 164
    chicks, 51–53
    dechlorinating, 121
    filling, 92
    ice, 113, 164
    puddles, 113
waterers, 52, 82
    cleaning, 90
    sanitizing, 93
wattles, 10–11, 67
    aging, 74
    health, 147, 153, 156, 162,
        168, 176
    sexing, 58
    temperature regulation, 30
weasels, 102, 106–107
weather, 137
weeds, 225
weight loss, 176
Welsummer
    climate, 20

speckled eggs, 139
wings
    health, 148, 157, 170, 172
    spreading, 163–164
    and temperature
        regulation, 30
winter, 136–137, 160
worms, 123, 175–177
    deworming, 176–177
    earthworms, 118
wry neck. *See* Stargazing
Wyandotte, 40
    climate, 18, 40
    comb, 15, 40
    egg color, 33
    eggs, 40
    feathers, 40
    meat, 40
    personality, 40

Y

yogurt, 60, 116, 157, 174
Yokohama
    comb, 15
yolk sac, 51

Z

zoning, 2–3